Early Childhood Playgrounds

The outdoor play environment has an integral role to play in a child's learning across the pivotal early childhood years. An outside space that is well designed maximises the use of space, ensuring the provision of areas which are enriching, stimulating and offer challenging play experiences to meet children's ongoing developmental needs. *Early Childhood Playgrounds* provides a step-by-step guide to planning, designing and creating an outdoor learning environment for young children.

Written by an experienced practitioner who has consulted on over 2,000 early childhood settings and schools internationally, this book considers all aspects of the outdoor learning environment and provides practical support on:

► following planning procedures and developing ideas for designs;
► encouraging a wide variety of play within a playground through the inclusion of quiet, open and active play areas;
► inspiring stimulating and challenging play;
► creating a natural environment that will provide interest and sustainability;
► including spaces for toddlers and babies;
► meeting playground requirements for children with additional needs.

This book will be fascinating reading for those studying early childhood and practitioners looking into the ways and means of setting up, improving or expanding their outdoor play facilities. It is also geared towards other disciplines, making it an essential guide for architects and planning professionals wanting to gain a greater understanding of play and the vital role it takes in meeting children's needs and development.

Prue Walsh is an early childhood graduate whose work has concentrated on creating effective and stimulating early childhood play environments. This work covers site assessment and the design of buildings and playgrounds in early childhood centres. Prue has also been involved in the development of public policy documents, most significantly the Best Practice Guidelines in Early Childhood Physical Environments.

Early Childhood Playgrounds

Planning an outside learning environment

Prue Walsh

Routledge
Taylor & Francis Group

LONDON AND NEW YORK

First published 2016
by Routledge
2 Park Square, Milton Park, Abingdon, Oxon OX14 4RN

and by Routledge
711 Third Avenue, New York, NY 10017

Routledge is an imprint of the Taylor & Francis Group, an informa business

British Library Cataloguing in Publication Data
A catalogue record for this book is available from the British Library

Library of Congress Cataloging in Publication Data
Names: Walsh, Prue, author.
Title: Early childhood playgrounds : planning an outside learning environment
/ Prue Walsh.
Description: Abingdon, Oxon ; New York, NY : Routledge, [2016]
Identifiers: LCCN 2015044022I ISBN 9781138859418 (hbk) I ISBN 9780415639279
(pbk.) I ISBN 9780203083628 (ebk)
Subjects: LCSH: Playgrounds—Design and construction. I Physical education
for children. I Early childhood education.
Classification: LCC GV424.5 .W35 2016 I DDC 711/.558083—dc23
LC record available at http://lccn.loc.gov/2015044022

ISBN: 978-1-138-85941-8 (hbk)
ISBN: 978-0-415-63927-9 (pbk)
ISBN: 978-0-203-08362-8 (ebk)

Typeset in Univers
by FiSH Books Ltd, Enfield

Contents

Contents

Acknowledgements

The upgrading and rewriting of this book could not have occurred without the feedback, support, dialogue and enthusiasm from a wide diversity of people both in Australia and overseas. They all share a great commitment to children and the provision of settings that enhance and enrich children's lives during their most formative years, within a markedly changing society.

Thanks go to the teachers and parents associated with early childhood services who I have had the privilege of working with during the upgrading or establishment of centres. I would also like to acknowledge the important feedback I have received from people involved in the development of early childhood centres. This book could not have been achieved without the professional commitment of early childhood professionals who have shared their experiences and concerns with me over the past 28 years. In particular I would like to acknowledge the continual support over long periods from early childhood professionals Bev Schneider and Jan Kan, particularly when facing challenging practices and politics.

I would also like to thank those individuals who have supported my work and provided invaluable insight into different cultural approaches and practices in the UK, the United States, Canada, Turkey, Denmark, Sweden, Finland, United Arab Emirates, Thailand, Hong Kong, Singapore, Indonesia and New Zealand. Most of all, I wish to acknowledge the support of Australians throughout every state and territory, including those from remote Aboriginal communities.

The rewriting of this book could not have occurred without my office being run so smoothly and supportively by Kerry Austin and previously Libby Needham. Throughout the years I have received vitally important support from Valerie Eldershaw through her clarification of information and assistance with editing my work. In more recent times I would like to acknowledge the work of Andrew Ross for saving the day for a tired writer by tidying up my text into the well-written book that it now is. I would also like to thank Bob James for his invaluable support with the planting section of this book and Stuart Mitchell for his help with design and construction queries.

Thanks also go to Julia Woodgate and Jacqui and John Younger for providing peaceful and quiet places to write, and to Vicky Jackson for her insight into children with special needs, and to Niki Buchan for nature play.

All drawings/sketches that appear in this book are concept only and are not drawn to scale. Implementation of any of these concepts should always be checked against your local playground standards and engineering advice sought if required.

Permissions

Acknowledgements are gratefully expressed for permission to use the following artwork:

I would like to acknowledge the wonderful drawings my husband John Walsh LFRAIA Architect did for this book. I could not have written this book without his support of the work I do and his patience and humour in persevering with a committed advocate towards designing physical environments that will support and extend children's learning through play during their most formative years.

Last but not least, special thanks go to my clients who have very generously permitted me to include photos of their playgrounds and children at play in this book: Alderley Kindergarten; Capital Hill Early Childhood Centre; Parliament House Australia; Chapel Hill Community Kindergarten; C&K Tarragindi War Memorial Kindergarten; Enka School in Istanbul; Kathy's House Family Day Care; Infants playground, Mater Dei School, Camden, a school for children with an intellectual disability; Tugulawa Early Education and Tricia King Photography. Thanks also to the staff of these child care centres and schools for your tireless efforts in securing the generous permission of the parents to have their children's photos included.

Preface

Early Childhood Playgrounds was first published in 1988 in response to needs expressed to me by teachers seeking support with the establishment, management and upgrading of early childhood centres. It is still in use.

This second edition of *Early Childhood Playgrounds* has been published in response to frequent requests from teachers in my native Australia and around the world for an updated version. It has taken into account their feedback on physical environments that promote learning through play and those that impede and constrain children.

It retains the commitment to writing from a practitioner's perspective, based on both research and practice findings, to provide a link for the critically needed multidisciplinary approach to planning and designing outdoor playgrounds.

Of course, in the intervening 25 years since the first edition was published, the context for early childhood playgrounds has changed dramatically. For example, in Australia, there has been a major shift from community-run centres and kindergartens to daycare provided in private and commercial centres. There has been a huge increase in the number of children in early childhood centres and in the number of hours they are in care as both parents work. More is known about the critical importance of play to a child's physical, mental and emotional development and learning in their early years.

This changing context makes the need for well-designed outdoor play spaces in early education centres even more important. And yet, it is my contention that during this time of rapid growth in children's centres the quality of physical environments for outdoor play has fallen away. Too often, outdoor play spaces have become the neglected physical areas in an early childhood centre. There continues to be a disturbing history of early childhood services being established without sufficient depth of understanding of children's needs and the types of facilities that will meet them. This reflects a lack of understanding and appreciation of how important outdoor play spaces should be for day-to-day teaching.

I hope this book will help to counter this trend, not least through showcasing images of well-designed and successful outdoor play spaces that have been provided in some early childhood centres.

While much has changed since the publication of the first edition of *Early Childhood Playgrounds* in 1988, one of the striking aspects of preparing an updated version is how ageless some of the writing on this topic has been in terms of expressing the fundamental need for children to play. For this reason, I have purposely included quotations from people whose writing has inspired and motived different aspects of my work over the years, whether it was written two, twenty or fifty years ago.

The overarching principle in this book is that in practice early childhood playground design must be addressed from the child's point of view. It is not the domain of the architect or landscape architect, a fixed equipment manufacturer or even the owner of a centre. First and foremost playgrounds are the domain of children. Their planning and design should be based on research and observation of how children play, and then on collaboration between teachers and a host of other disciplines to ensure that outdoor play spaces are designed so that children get the best possible start in life.

Prue Walsh
2015

CHAPTER 1

Setting the scene

1.1 Outside learning environments: under threat?

The reduction in outside play is a feature of life for children living in developed countries in the twenty-first century, and there is deep concern about the consequences this change will have for child development (for example, see Moss 2012). This book acknowledges that there is a context of a general angst around the lack of outdoor play, and provision for outdoor play, but focuses solely on outdoor play spaces attached to children's centres, nurseries and other early childhood facilities. As more and more children continue to live in urban areas, some children's only real sensory experience of outdoor play will be at the playground attached to one of these facilities. Ensuring a high quality outdoor play experience across all centres is critical to providing a level playing field for children in their early years. These spaces need to be thought about and designed differently to a playground in a public park, which would normally cater for a much wider range of ages.

This idea is not new. In 1977 Sybil Kritchevsky and Elizabeth Prescott wrote that:

> The higher the quality of space in a centre, the more likely were teachers to be sensitive and friendly in their manner toward children, to encourage children in their self-chosen activities, and to teach consideration for the rights and. feelings of self and others. Where spatial quality was low, children were less likely to be involved and interested, and teachers more likely to be neutral or insensitive in their manner, to use larger amounts of guidance and restriction, and to teach arbitrary rules of social living.

Despite the importance of these spaces, there are clear signs that they are failing to meet children's needs and are the 'forgotten spaces' which are poorly understood when it comes to designing an early childhood centre.

There are a number of reasons to be concerned. First, as intimated above, children's safety has become a prime consideration in the developed world. This anxiety has leached into playground design. The outcome in practice has been an over-zealous approach to safety that limits children's play and is holding back their development.

Rather than seeking to eliminate risk in play – which is as impossible to achieve as devising a risk-free life – a better approach would be to seek a balance, where children's developmental needs are put first. The British play experts David Ball, Tim Gill and Bernard Spiegal (2012) put it like this:

> Risk management in play provision involves balancing risks and benefits in a strategic way. Since the reason for providing play opportunities is their benefit to children and young people, the starting point – the most important consideration – for risk assessment and decision-making should be an understanding of the benefit that the provision offers.

Nowhere is this approach needed more than the early childhood years when children are at their peak period of laying the foundations of their life skills and will extend, fine-tune and master all areas of their development. Injury data within Australia and elsewhere has shown that the peak period of injuries occur with newly mobile toddlers who have just mastered their upright position, are extending and developing their perceptions of space, have an overriding curiosity and discovery, and are seeking but not always knowing how to develop friendships.

Throughout early childhood, children use play to master overall body coordination, to learn to fit in with other children, and to pursue challenges and enjoy the satisfaction of achieving new skills. An element of risk taking is integral to all these aspects of development.

And yet, in Australia and other parts of the developed world, playground design has been increasingly driven by what appear to be commercial and litigation interests that have exploited underlying anxieties around risk and safety, and been counterproductive and harmful to meeting children's needs through play.

Australia's National Injury Surveillance system was set up in 1988. Early childhood playgrounds were found to have a low number of injuries and were therefore not prioritised for further analysis or in-depth research. Unfortunately, rather than being used as an enabling information source, the data gathered for all playgrounds has been used as a justification for imposing unnecessary restrictions on early childhood play spaces.

Regrettably, this has tended to be driven by a fear of litigation rather than a proper assessment of children's play needs. The outcome has been restrictive playgrounds that inhibit play and a denial to children of the benefits of enriching – and, yes, risk-taking – outdoor play. As Tom Jambor writes: 'We have technically done a fine job of setting national guidelines to make children's playgrounds safer. But, in the process we have factored out the play value, especially with regard to challenge needs.' (Jambor 1996).

An overemphasis on safety rather than a careful management of risk is not the only threat to children's outside play spaces. The price of land, escalating building costs and poorly sited centres on non-standard sites has meant that the outdoor play space is too often treated as a poor afterthought. This is indicative of little understanding of children's needs and what they actually require to thrive in outdoor spaces. The consequence is cramped, poorly designed spaces that fail to provide a suitable environment for young children to develop and thrive. Too often they end up with play pens rather than playgrounds!

The combination of safety concerns and increasing constraints on spatial provision has markedly constrained the diversity of play opportunities being provided in outdoor play spaces, with consequences including less focused and more antisocial play.

And yet, this is not the whole story. Since the publication of the first edition of *Early Childhood Playgrounds* in 1988 much has been learned about the value of play for children's development, and the importance of outdoor spaces to help enable this. Concern about the lack of access of children to nature – expressed most cogently by Richard Louv (2005) with his notion of 'nature deficit disorder' – has tapped into deep-seated parental anxieties about over-exposing children to technology and sedentary activities at the expense of outdoor play.

There are also some outstanding examples of outside learning environments in children's centres to counter the poor provision criticised above. The photos in this book highlight what is possible. These play spaces are designed to reflect the needs of the children who use them, as well as responding positively to the opportunities and constraints of the site where they are located. Crucially, they reflect a multidisciplinary approach that recognises the importance of putting children's needs first and incorporating early childhood expertise from the start.

Creating generous outside play spaces that put children's needs at their heart should be seen as an investment that will reap dividends. Play is critical to the overall rounded development of children, who will become the adults of the future. It is therefore essential that substantial, inspiring and well designed outdoor play spaces are provided to compensate for the lost fields, open pathways and large back gardens of past eras.

1.2 Why outdoor play is important

An effective early childhood centre playground is an area of constant daily use during the prime developmental years of a child's life, and will be the setting for a high degree of focused, concentrated play. For many children it will be their main outdoor experience during the most formative years of their life.

However, too often playgrounds are designed by adults without the experience or real understanding of working with children and the evolving depth of knowledge of children's play and developmental needs and the type of environment required. As Roger Hart puts it: 'Most people who care about child development know nothing about design, and most people who know design know nothing about child development'. (Roger Hart quoted in Ruppel Shell, 1994.)

To meet the developmental needs of young children, it is essential that play spaces are flexible, adaptable and sensory rich spaces set in a framework of space that will allow for a degree of

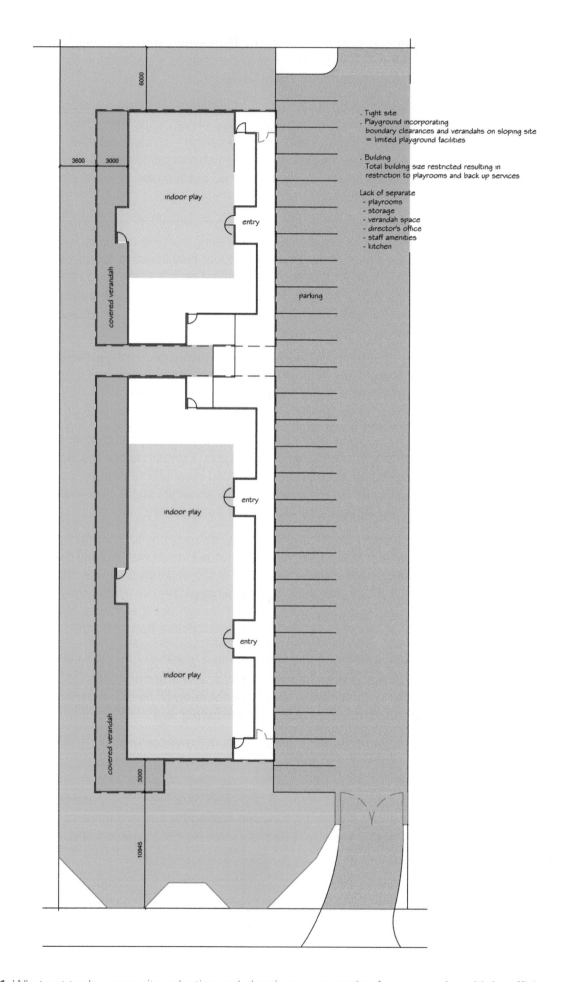

Figure 1.1 What not to do – poor site selection and planning: an example of a narrow site with insufficient outdoor space

evolving change and the spatial provision to allow this to occur. These principles not only come from practice, but are endorsed by the work of the Russian developmental psychologist, Lev Vygotsky, who emphasised that each child has a 'zone of proximal development'. In practice, this means providing spaces that act as a supportive framework for child development through play, that have a range of different play spaces within an adaptable setting, with a dominance of natural environments and adaptable settings will provide the flexibility needed to keep the ongoing process of stimulation and arousal of interest in play maintained.

For the provision of play spaces to be effective, the design must be based on an understanding of children's play and developmental needs. If a designer truly uses this premise as her or his starting point, then the space will look different from most adult perceptions of outdoor play spaces, such as most public playgrounds.

Each chapter in this book summarises the specific play and developmental needs that the different play areas should aim to fulfil. Early childhood educators and designers should remind themselves constantly of why outdoor play is fundamental for children, apart from the simple right that they have to play because it is what they want and need to do. Play helps children improve their:

- ▶ cognitive development (including language skills, problem solving and independent learning skills, self-efficacy, gaining perspective, representational skills, memory and creativity);
- ▶ physical health and development (including physiological, cardiovascular and fine and gross motor skills development as well as increased physical activity);
- ▶ mental health, happiness and emotional wellbeing (including building confidence, improved child–parent attachments, coping with stress, tackling anxieties and phobias, aiding recovery in therapeutic contexts, and alleviating the symptoms of ADHD for some children);
- ▶ social development (including working with others, sharing, negotiating and appreciating others' points of view);
- ▶ risk management and resilience through experiencing and responding to unexpected, challenging situations.

(The Play Return by Tim Gill (2014) for the Children's Play Policy Council)

1.3 Designing outdoor play spaces for children

The design characteristics that underpin an effective playground are listed below. They are geared specifically to running an early childhood programme and meeting the developmental needs of children. Incorporation of space combined with paying attention to these design characteristics will assist in sustaining children's interest and empower them in their play-learning. A safe environment is crucial, but this does not need to be at the expense of providing a stimulating outdoor play space. It is also worth remembering that:

> No playground is achieved by play apparatus alone, however well thought through it may be. This is often forgotten, and it may well be this very forgetfulness that is the cause of our failure.
>
> (Richard Dattner 1969)

The characteristics below are reflected throughout this guide as they cut across all the different play settings.

1.3.1 Space

Underpinning the provision of space which will assist children's independence and the provision of a wide variety of different forms of potential play opportunities is an essential foundation to the provision of outdoor play. Hence, the provision of effective space is included in many sections of this book.

1.3.2 Variety of spaces

Ideally a children's centre playground will be an interlinked, compatible series of spaces, each with a different play purpose to reflect the needs of the children. Most of this book is devoted to describing how to design these different spaces – natural, open, quiet, active – in detail. Each space should suggest, but not dictate, use. It is important to keep in mind that, within this overall variety, the physical environment should also create an identity that helps to foster a sense of ownership, attachment and familiarity.

There should be a complexity to this variety that helps children to master a range of skills. The spaces that are needed vary from open running spaces where children gather with friends to move with speed to nooks, crannies and hiding spots where they can retreat when they want to be on their own or to recover when they are tired.

1.3.3 Sensory richness

Children's experience of the environment is inherent to their exploration and understanding of the world. The process of touching, tasting, listening, smelling and exploring within the environment starts when we are babies. The richer the experience for babies and children, the greater their exploration, discovery, enjoyment and understanding of the diversity of the world in which they live. There are many subtle ways of providing a rich sensory outdoor play space, for example varied planting, unstructured play materials, and different textures, shapes, spaces and surfaces.

1.3.4 Scale

A marked variation to the scale of spaces needs to be provided. This includes:

▶ entry spaces to define a welcoming part of the play area such as a vine-covered arch leading to a quiet nook;
▶ open running spaces that assist access from one end of the playground to the other;
▶ large group spaces such as a hub where children can gather;
▶ small spaces such as nooks and crannies where a child can sit and reflect or share with a friend.

Figure 1.2 Alderley Kindergarten: the joy of sensory exploration and discovery

1.3.5 Linkage, flow and legibility

The way these varied spaces are linked should support a natural progression and flow of play. For example:

▶ an open area with space to run and mounds to scale;
▶ an open area leading to a hub and sandpit linked to a shallow watercourse;
▶ an active area where adaptable fixtures can be incorporated (for example, a deck with cleat rails on the underside to allow for planks and ladders to be added).

These links need to make the play spaces accessible for a range of age levels and abilities, while at the same time allowing for easy observation and supervision by teachers.

Organising the play spaces into a legible pattern can help to make children feel at home and allow for a natural progression and flow of play.

1.3.6 Natural features

Children prefer a natural setting for their play. As Peter Heseltine repeatedly observes and notes: 'It continues to be startling how often the research and the children's own choice stresses the importance of the natural environment – and how often its importance is ignored in practice.' (In Jambor 1996, Dimensions of Play: reflections and directions.)

Early childhood education also stresses the need to teach sustainability from a young age, and it is vital that children have access to natural elements as part of this learning. Designers should exploit any opportunities to incorporate as many natural features as possible such as interesting landforms, watercourses, trees, low-level and high-level plants. The provision of subtle natural stimuli, particularly through planting, provides an ongoing catalyst to children's play.

1.3.7 Flexible, open-ended play

Children's joy of discovery needs a flexible space that can be used in multiple diverse ways. They might initially use a fixed climbing structure that has one set use. But once they have mastered it they will soon tire of it, which ends up making this equipment a waste of time and money. Contrast this with the flexibility of a low flat deck with a cleat rail on the underside to link planks and ladders to, or a series of stepped decks large enough for groups of children to play on, climb between or have a hidey space underneath, which allows for open-ended play. A flexible space also helps teachers to make subtle adaptations to the environment to sustain children's interest and to stimulate their development.

A few permanent fixtures are important because they provide a sense of home and identity. But they need to be designed so that they have a high level of potentially adaptable use within the area.

1.4 The role of the teacher

Teachers of young children have a determining role to play in the provision of a wide variety of play opportunities. They are trained to observe, evaluate and assess children's play and needs and to provide support and encouragement when need is indicated. Part of their role is to enable children to explore and discover through play and to consolidate their skills. It should not depend on directive handling of children and a structured outdoor classroom programme, which are teaching methods used for older children at school. Using their observations, they will vary play options within the playground each day when needed.

Access to a natural setting, loose parts and junk materials allows for subtle differentiation to create different configurations of movable materials, areas to explore and materials to be manipulated by children to accommodate their ideas. This needs to be an ongoing practice of extending existing play options or adding new ones. Often the variations are slight, just enough to motivate children, but not to confuse or over stimulate them. The teacher's skill is to provide challenge and increase the complexity of different settings in gradual stages, so that a child's motivation, active engagement and interest are sustained.

Enabling these subtle changes to the physical environment creates new experiences and levels of challenge that stimulate an ongoing passage of exploration and discovery for a child. Lev Vygotsky, the Russian developmental psychologist, expressed this as each child having a zone of 'proximal development' (2014; Fred Newman and Lois Holzman, Lev Vygotsky: revolutionary scientist). This refers to a level of development that a child can achieve with support or 'scaffolding' provided by their teachers.

The teacher will often stand back and observe children engrossed in play, not interfering but letting them know they approve of what they are doing. There will be moments when teachers may realise that children are creating undue frustration or putting themselves at unnecessary risk. At these times they will need to mediate, handle with care and briefly explain the use of equipment. Each time this must be dealt with in a considered and clear manner often gently, sometimes firmly and, as children get older, with clear reasoning for the intervention.

The physical environment therefore underpins effective teaching practice, and teachers must engage in any proposals to redesign, amend or create a play space from scratch. Their insight into the development needs of children must take centre-stage during the design process. If expertise cannot be sought from other early childhood experts to convey needs and future usage, then teachers must show leadership and require that they are involved. Otherwise, they will be frustrated by working in play spaces that are ill-suited to effective teaching practice.

Figure 1.3 Enka Schools in Istanbul: the teacher provides support and reassurance through shared experiences

1.5 How to use this book

This is a book about practice, and about designing outdoor play spaces that children will enjoy and that will be effective in fostering discovery, exploration and an expansion of knowledge to support their development and education. Crucially, it focuses on designing the outdoor play spaces of children's centres and nursery facilities including those for children with special needs. Throughout the terms early childhood centres, children's centres and nurseries are used interchangeably to refer to places of childcare for children of pre-school age.

It is directed primarily at early childhood practitioners to help them understand and influence the design of play spaces that will help children develop. It will also assist centre owners and managers, management committees and design professionals (architects, landscape architects, urban planners) who seek to create more wonderful outdoor teaching spaces and offers strategies for how all disciplines can and need to work together. Developers of centres and sites without any experienced early childhood input will in practice critically need support. The guidelines, suggestions and ideas in the book can be tailored to suit a range of budgets, sizes, spaces and climates.

Use the book in conjunction with relevant local standards and statutory requirements to guide the development of a future playground, to overhaul an existing space, or to challenge providers to do better.

CHAPTER 2

Planning an outside learning environment

2.1 Why planning is important

Arvid Bengtsson wisely wrote in Bengtsson 1970, p. 23: 'We too often forget that planning for play is very much a question of communication'.

To ensure that an early childhood centre will be viable, sustainable and effective at meeting children's needs and teaching requirements, a careful planning process must be undertaken, which extends from site selection through to the development of plans and provision of facilities. Effective planning will ensure that a greater depth of understanding of children's play is achieved by all participants who are involved in the planning process. To quote Helen Bilton, 'outdoor provision has to be seen as a long-term project which cannot be rushed'.

The day-to-day management of a centre can also be assisted by a well-planned physical environment, which provides low-key, but often very practical, support for children and teachers, such as easy access to loose parts.

Integral to the planning process is using the services of parties with early childhood professional expertise who have a deep and informed understanding of children's overall development and the type of play facilities they will need. Outdoor play facilities that have been planned and developed without this expertise have resulted in major shortfalls in playground provision.

Another important benefit of planning the overall site is to avoid ad hoc development. This is where a centre manager or developer makes incremental changes to an outdoor play space, usually to save money in the short term, without consideration of the longer-term implications for play provision, risk management and ongoing maintenance costs. This kind of unplanned development is a major problem occurring in many centres and is one of the most repeated concerns with the use of public money. In contrast, professional early childhood-based master-planning should always be undertaken with initial planning and costs being established to ensure that this becomes and informed submission for parties when seeking funding. In practice this approach will provide proof of the validity of outcomes being sought. Staging of master planning may only lead to partial funding being received, however, in practice it has been found that taking this approach is the catalyst to speedier implementation. Staged with staged development will provide quality outcomes and eliminate misguided use of funding with long-term developmental benefits to children.

Of course, pulling all the necessary funding together before a project commences can be challenging. In the likelihood of full funding not being available, potential staged implementation should occur so that the full plan can be achieved as and when money becomes available.

The process of seeking finance for a quality outdoor play space is an important advocacy on behalf of children. It helps funding bodies (and often government) to understand the true costs involved in developing a playground, and the variations in price depending on the advantages and constraints of the site and the work carried out previously.

2.2 Assess the site

The development of any early childhood centre playground must begin with site assessment. This needs to be based primarily on meeting children's needs and ensuring that the site will have the capacity to cope with these needs while also establishing its commercial viability.

The relative strengths and weaknesses of the proposed site must be assessed, and these will help to provide the basis on which to design. It is essential that this detailed evaluation of the site is carried out prior to the purchase of any property to ensure the financial goals of the owners do not compromise delivery of services for children. For existing centres, it is essential to establish if the current building/s will meet children's needs and to ensure an integrated indoor/outdoor environment can be achieved.

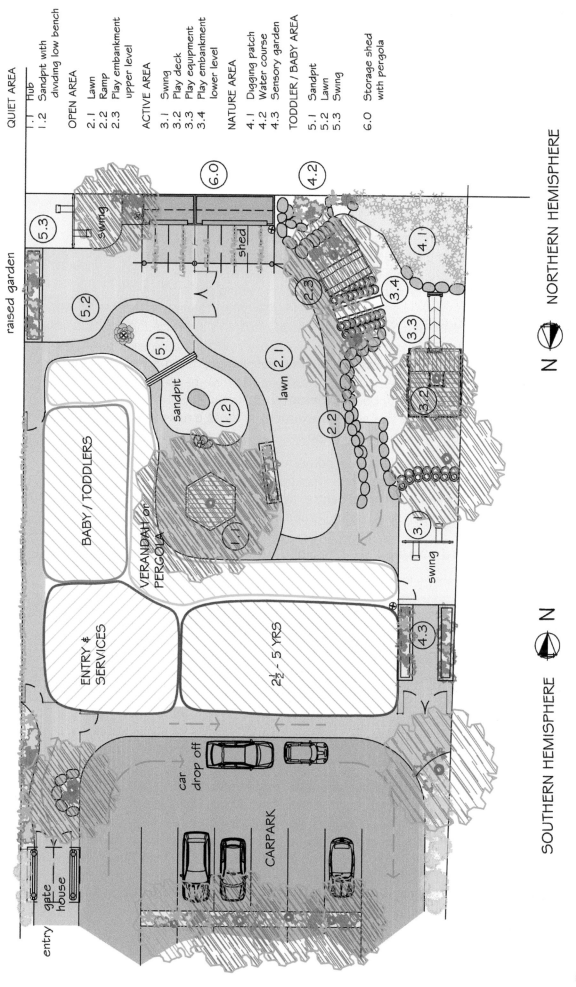

QUIET AREA
1.1 Hub
1.2 Sandpit with
dividing low bench

OPEN AREA
2.1 Lawn
2.2 Ramp
2.3 Play embankment
upper level

ACTIVE AREA
3.1 Swing
3.2 Play deck
3.3 Play equipment
3.4 Play embankment
lower level

NATURE AREA
4.1 Digging patch
4.2 Water course
4.3 Sensory garden

TODDLER / BABY AREA
5.1 Sandpit
5.2 Lawn
5.3 Swing

6.0 Storage shed
with pergola

SOUTHERN HEMISPHERE   N   N   NORTHERN HEMISPHERE

Figure 2.1 Effective playground planning: large playground, easy access visually and physically between inside and outside of the building. Cars are separated and easily accessible under supervision from the building but not intrusive or in conflict to play facilities

Comprehensive site assessment will also establish whether there is sufficient spatial provision for the potential number of children is realistic to ensure that it will offer a rich and diverse outside learning environment. It is important to remember that high-density use of space is more likely to result in less focused play and more anti-social aggressive behaviour – the range of play options will be insufficient to meet the needs of the children and their varied interests.

Careful assessment of the site should involve taking into account clear and realistic ideas about the projected use of the areas. Without this, too often, the provision of children's play and teacher's programming needs are markedly constrained.

2.2.1 Location

The proposed site for a new or existing centre should be evaluated for the following:

▶ Is it located in an area where there is community demand for early childhood care?
▶ Does it/will it fulfil a community need?
▶ Is it easy to walk, cycle or use public transport to get there?
▶ Is it suitably located for safe drop-off by car and for providing parking?
▶ Does the location provide viewing access to an adjoining park, a view out to sea or water, or to the surrounding neighbourhood, which will enhance children's appreciation and understanding of the space?
▶ What is the adjacent land being used for: industrial, residential, commercial or something else?
▶ Are there residential neighbours to be considered?
▶ What was previously located on this site: for example, is there a risk of toxicity from a former petrol station or reclaimed waste disposal land?

All too often centres are established on busy corners or roads to increase exposure as a commercial means for filling the centre. These locations will threaten the quality of the programme being run in an early childhood centre. Inhibiting constraints include the shape and form of the playground, noise pollution, traffic fumes and traffic volume and danger.

2.2.2 Space, size and shape

When assessing size and shape look foremost at the proposed number of children to be accommodated within the space, and take account of potential future growth.

Australian regulations require that early childhood centres must have a minimum of $7m^2$ of outdoor space per child; verandahs attached to buildings count as outdoor space (ACECQA, 2014). However, it is unclear why this figure has been chosen. Significant practitioner experience suggests that the following provision of space allows for an essential area of sufficient size to ensure a diverse, safe and convivial outdoor play setting (Walsh 2006):

▶ 75 place centre – $15m^2$ per child ($1125m^2$ minimum total);
▶ 40 place centre – $20m^2$ per child ($800m^2$ minimum total);
▶ 25 place centre – $25m^2$ per child ($625m^2$ minimum total).

These figures are based on a careful assessment of the playground space of over 800 centres in Australia and from information gathered from at least twenty five plans given to me when working overseas. The spaces listed above were selected based on teachers and managers of centres reporting that these amounts provide sound outside spatial areas for children's needs. Interestingly, these figures mirror those published in the early 1970s by the Australian Preschool Association (now Early Childhood Australia), which also recommended a minimum spatial provision of $15m^2$ per child. Over time, this figure has been slowly whittled down by questionable advice provided by childcare regulators.

Another factor relating to the effectiveness of spatial provision that has emerged from consistent feedback from early childhood teachers relates to the shape of the site and the need for this to

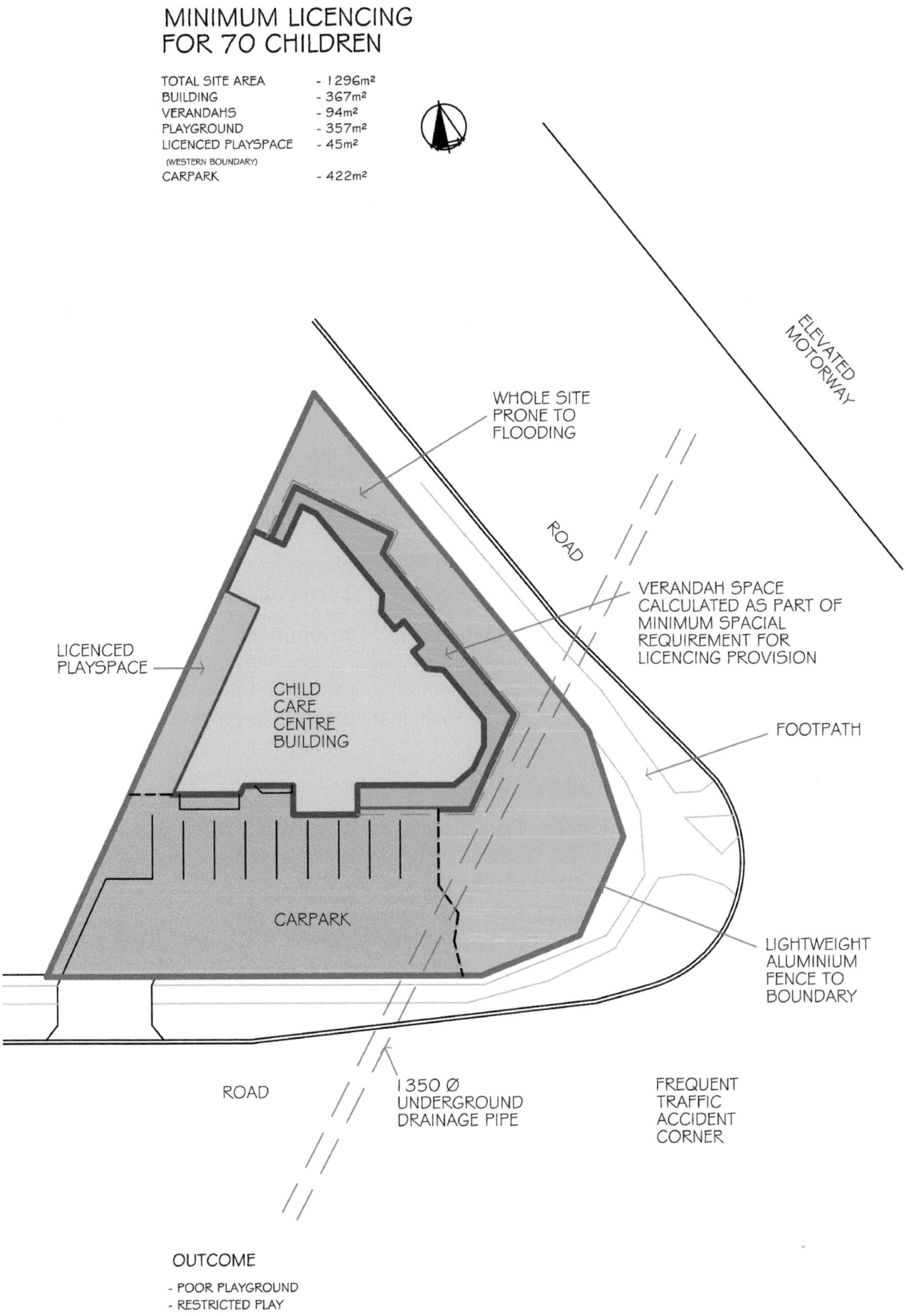

MINIMUM LICENCING FOR 70 CHILDREN

TOTAL SITE AREA	- 1296m²
BUILDING	- 367m²
VERANDAHS	- 94m²
PLAYGROUND	- 357m²
LICENCED PLAYSPACE	- 45m²
(WESTERN BOUNDARY)	
CARPARK	- 422m²

WHOLE SITE PRONE TO FLOODING

ELEVATED MOTORWAY

ROAD

VERANDAH SPACE CALCULATED AS PART OF MINIMUM SPACIAL REQUIREMENT FOR LICENCING PROVISION

LICENCED PLAYSPACE

CHILD CARE CENTRE BUILDING

FOOTPATH

CARPARK

LIGHTWEIGHT ALUMINIUM FENCE TO BOUNDARY

ROAD

1350 Ø UNDERGROUND DRAINAGE PIPE

FREQUENT TRAFFIC ACCIDENT CORNER

OUTCOME

- POOR PLAYGROUND
- RESTRICTED PLAY

Figure 2.2 Poor site selection and planning: small restricted site with poorly laid out building resulting in insufficient playground space leading to insufficient play opportunities. Located on a busy corner creating noise and fumes across the site

be carefully assessed. An effective site is either a squat rectangular or a large square site, or an irregular shaped site which is still easy to supervise. Long, narrow spaces, particularly when incorporating boundary clearances, often create problems for the ability to provide access between indoor and outdoor areas, but noticeably they constrain the planning of the layout. Narrow boundary clearances should not be included in the usable playground space as they are difficult to supervise, put children at greater risk and limit potential play inclusions.

2.2.3 Buildings and existing playgrounds

Whether existing or proposed, buildings should be appraised in relation to the boundaries and playground to ensure the maximum use of land without impeding outdoor play spaces.

The following should be assessed:

▶ the state of existing buildings and their viability to work effectively: appraisal of room sizes, existing storage facilities, accessibility and staff facilities;
▶ the capacity for the number of children currently accommodated and the proposed future number;
▶ the implications of extending the building and the use of the remaining section of the site without detrimentally affecting outdoor play;
▶ the capacity of the site to be altered without intruding on existing and/or future outdoor play spaces;
▶ establish whether any of the items above need to be replaced or are going to inhibit and be intrusive to utilising the maximum potential amount of space available.

It is also essential to check federal/central, state and local government building requirements, for example, boundary clearances, street access and car parking requirements. Also check whether these will place major constraints on the use of available space and if they will intrude so markedly on children's outdoor play areas that it would be unviable to provide quality facilities on the site.

Before re-planning existing playgrounds the following features should be assessed:

▶ position of all existing equipment and fixed structures, for example sheds, climbing structures, swings, pools, digging patches and sandpits, retaining walls and taps;
▶ siting of garden beds, large trees and shrubs;
▶ siting of fences, double and single gates;
▶ position of the building in relation to the playground.

2.2.4 Access

Consider the following:

▶ swift access to and from the building and playground for large numbers, for example 25 children and supervising teachers;
▶ provision of facilities that allow for independent access by children – both viewing and pedestrian;
▶ easy entry from the street and car park: is there access to the building for mothers and children? Does access cut across the centre of the playground and inhibit the layout of space;
▶ gate access for delivery trucks;
▶ properly designed car parks (if required) so that children can alight safely from a car onto a footpath. The lack of the provision of a pathway is a known cause of children being severely injured and, in some cases, being run over by reversing cars.

2.2.5 Landform, topography and soil

The playground site should be surveyed to gain a clear picture of the land's natural slopes, contours, variations in height and soil type.

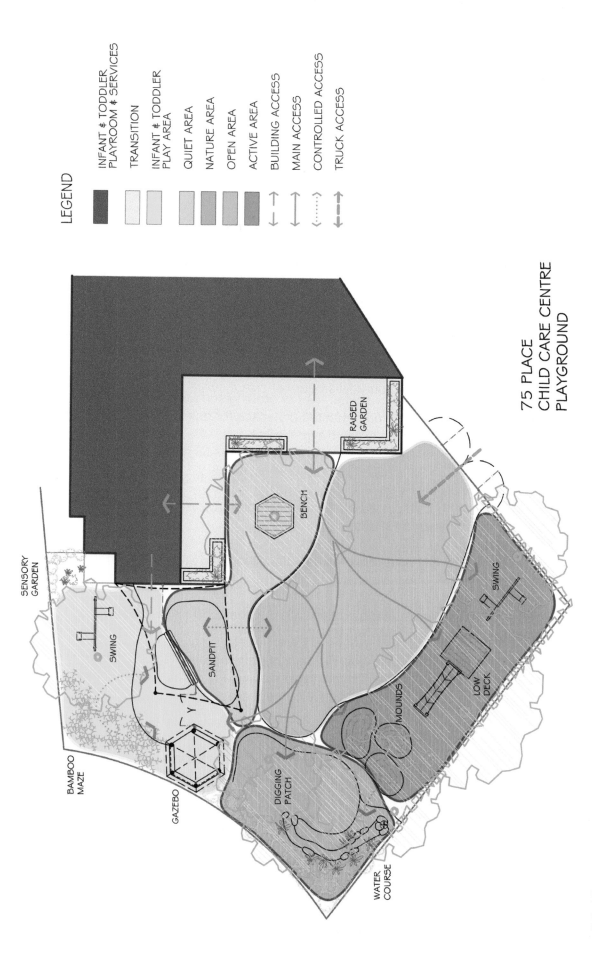

LEGEND

INFANT & TODDLER PLAYROOM & SERVICES
TRANSITION
INFANT & TODDLER PLAY AREA
QUIET AREA
NATURE AREA
OPEN AREA
ACTIVE AREA
BUILDING ACCESS
MAIN ACCESS
CONTROLLED ACCESS
TRUCK ACCESS

SENSORY GARDEN

BAMBOO MAZE

GAZEBO

SWING

SANDPIT

DIGGING PATCH

WATER COURSE

MOUNDS

LOW DECK

SWING

BENCH

RAISED GARDEN

75 PLACE
CHILD CARE CENTRE
PLAYGROUND

Figure 2.3 Allocation of space and access: initial playground design showing open, quiet and active areas designed for specific forms of play as well as a smaller adjoining playground area to allow for social interaction and support between children as well as ease of supervision and support between all spaces

For full play potential to be realised some areas of almost flat land are needed. While these spaces provide ample opportunity for a variety of play, they can become boring and may require earthworks to create mounds or other spatial variations. Steep embankments can be an advantage, but when they take up the major part of a whole site they inhibit the diversity of play. In practice, a generous spatial provision that would accommodate a steep embankment as well as providing sufficient open running space and steep climbs is an advantage.

Earthworks of steep sites and flat sites will create more effective playgrounds. Invariably, major additional costs can be involved when earthworks are required and so the need for earthwork should be established early in the planning process as it can be a major determining factor as to whether the site will be viable due to the costs that can be incurred. Minimum government licensing requirements should only be seen as that as they potentially provide insufficient space for an effective playground.

The depth and nature of the top- and sub-soil should be assessed for future planting and as a surface material. Eroded areas will rapidly deteriorate with heavy use, so planning must take this into account to prevent recurrent maintenance problems.

2.2.6 Orientation and climate

Good planning will utilise the best features of climate and protect children from the worst. Where possible choose a northerly facing (or southerly facing in the northern hemisphere) aspect to aid planning and assessment of climatic effects in the playground.

Avoid open playgrounds without trees or shelter, wet or eroding surfaces caused by heavy rainfall and poor soils, windy playgrounds with no protected dry space for quiet play, wind-blown sandpits, and hot and arid, or cold and sunless playgrounds.

Climatic factors to consider are:

▶ monthly and yearly rainfall;
▶ extremes in temperature: in cold climates the siting of a playground on the top of a ridge may not be suitable as wind speeds are greater;
▶ wind: velocity and direction;
▶ sun: its position during the day when children use the playground and during different times of the year to gain the benefits of winter sunlight and to protect against hot summer burning sunlight;
▶ specific climatic conditions, for example proximity to the coast, humidity, valley winds, cyclonic weather, aridity and drought.

Ideally these factors should be considered during the initial site assessment stage prior to procurement or development of any site. The cost of rectifying any of these factors may be significant and needs to be calculated into the development costs.

2.2.7 Existing vegetation

As much of the existing vegetation as possible should be kept, as this is a vital component of a playground. Take note of tree and shrub height, canopy, condition and species if possible. Use the services of an arborist to carefully evaluate the existing vegetation, and to ensure that well-established trees are viable in the long term, and can be used for shade and to break up the different spaces on the site.

2.2.8 Drainage and water

The topography plan can be used to help assess patterns of natural drainage, areas of watershed and the depth of the water table. Creeks, pools, swamps and natural springs all need to be taken into account; the plan may be able to use these constructively for outdoor play if spatial provision allows.

2.2.9 Existing and proposed services

Services should be noted and their location recorded for their impact on site use, accessibility for maintenance, and to prevent damage during playground construction. The main ones are:

► roads, parking areas and footpaths adjacent to the playground;
► drainage and sewerage lines or pits, gas mains, electricity cables, telecommunication lines and water;
► taps, water channels, agricultural pipe drains and storm-water systems;
► fire truck entry;
► make sure that the inclusion of any of these items supports rather than impedes effective use of the future playground.

2.2.10 Adjoining land uses

These should be recorded as they will influence playground design. The new plan should:

► block out obtrusive neighbouring elements: common ones are high factory walls, unsightly yards, noisy polluting roads, high unit developments and noisy shopping centres;
► utilise any attractive views and neighbouring trees, which are areas of aesthetic beauty and interest.

2.2.11 Specific community needs

The needs of different community groups should always be considered and may need accommodating. Children who have cramped urban home spaces rely far more heavily on public open spaces and natural spaces. Early childhood centres have an enormous role to play in providing this space to allow children the opportunity to accommodate skills as diverse as those which will support the development of gross motor skills and facilitate the sort of group play that may not be able to be accommodated in their home environment or immediate environment. In country or rural areas additional space can aid socialisation of isolated children who are used to feeling more at ease in larger spaces which offer greater freedom of movement which may have cultural significance, notably for Australia Aboriginal children.

2.3 Establish a master-planning group

A multidisciplinary approach to design – including close communication, collaboration and sharing responsibility – will be required for the complex task of designing an outside learning environment where children's play can flourish. The most practical way of achieving this is to set up a small, balanced planning group/sub-committee representing specific areas of expertise and need. Open balanced communication between the multidisciplinary team and others with transdisciplinary skills will underpin effective planning.

Ideally the multidisciplinary planning group should include:

► a trained and experienced early childhood educator/professional with experience in running an outdoor programme, or who may have been involved with the design of previous centres. This is essential to ensure that children's needs underpin the planning;
► a management representative, for example, the centre's owner;
► a parent or community representative;
► one or two early childhood teachers currently employed in the centre/service.

Additional balanced informed advice should be sought and provided by other professionals in collaboration with the planning group to cover the following areas where needs are indicated:

► town planner to establish local planning requirements;
► landscape architects: check if they have done any training related to children's play or have had experience working with the planning of playgrounds for early childhood centres as

distinct from public parks, as these spaces need to be interpreted and designed differently. If these skills are present they could well play an important role in the planning team;
▶ engineer to oversee issues such as drainage, structural walls and site specific requirements;
▶ sound and traffic engineer to establish the intrusiveness of adjoining properties and surroundings.

2.4 Tasks of the planning group

The following list is intended as a rough guide to the duties of a planning group, from early planning through to completion of work.

2.4.1 Manage consultation

For existing centres, the planning group should take into consideration the view of the teachers and any advisory reports and letters regarding the playground, as well as any state and local government regulations.

For new centres, the planning group should read and discuss any relevant literature from the parent organisation and discuss the master-plan with them. State and local government regulations should also be considered noting the all too often strengths and weaknesses of these documents to establish if a more generous solution can be achieved.

In both instances the centre's current advisory teacher should be approached for further information. This input can save time by drawing the group's attention to official requirements and problems, as well as stimulating additional ideas and solutions.

Check if any previous plans exist as these could be adapted to help save money.

2.4.2 Appoint a professional playground designer

Write a design brief (that is, an explanation of what you want) and select an early childhood professional designer or landscape architect with knowledge and experience of early childhood centre needs and planning solutions. Once appointed they should be recommended to the centre's management committee.

It is essential that the preferred designer visit the site to discuss the list of needs with the planning group, and consolidate the design brief prior to commencing work. The planning group should request and approve a written submission from the preferred designer based on the brief, which confirms the extent of services and professional fees. Once approved, write a letter of appointment to the playground designer and set out the agreed conditions of engagement.

At all times the planning group must adhere to the advice provided by experienced early childhood experts to ensure the best outcomes for children.

2.4.3 Oversee the preparation of the master-plan

The appointed designer will need to draw a master-plan of their proposed outdoor play space. At the least this plan should:

▶ be based on an accurate site assessment;
▶ reflect aspirations set out in the design brief;
▶ include a record of existing features;
▶ include a sketch plan of existing structures for further consideration (suggest drawn to scale 1:100): detailed drawing to a larger scale will be needed for some areas, particularly where child safety is concerned, for example all climbing equipment, swings, sandpits and freefall safety zones (barkchip);
▶ include a planting schedule (if required);
▶ estimate the overall cost and, if necessary, recommend how the plan could be implemented in stages, subject to funding.

Once the master-plan has been agreed by the planning group they should recommend it to the management committee for approval.

2.4.4 Appoint contractors

Management and teacher representatives need to be party to these discussions. They are likely to involve:

- issuing a call for tenders;
- assessing responses;
- selecting a preferred contractor/s;
- agreeing a contract.

2.4.5 Manage implementation

The planning group should give careful consideration to appointing an experienced person to be in charge of the project implementation and to work collaboratively with the playground designer and building contractor/s. Issues to be aware of include:

- unauthorised alterations to approved plans: these should be avoided at all times;
- proposed changes to the approved plans: these need to be discussed with the planning group, and in particular the early childhood educator/consultant who was involved in designing the playground to ensure that the changes would not compromise how the children will use the space;
- existing plants: ensure they are protected during construction.

Periodic site inspections should be arranged to oversee implementation and to ensure compliance with plans and government requirements. In particular look out for:

- incorrect siting of equipment such as the climbing structures and swings being incorrectly placed, or positioned too close to other fixed structures and presenting a major safety hazard;
- work signed off by contractors, but only partly completed;
- shoddy workmanship that could expose children to injury, such as exposed concrete footings (easy to trip over), or rough timber finishes (lead to splinters and cuts);
- building materials and equipment left on site after completion of the work.

2.4.6 Evaluate the project

Close evaluation of how children use the completed space is essential for the ongoing professional development of everyone involved so that a broader and clearer body of knowledge is shared and accrued for future projects.

A key feature in the evaluation should be teacher feedback on how children use the play spaces: what is sustaining their interest, and what is not, and what modifications may be required? Particular care should be given to ensuring that the original planner of the playground, whether it be a person with early childhood transdisciplinary skills or a landscape architect, is provided with this feedback.

2.4.7 In summary

'Good spaces for children (and adults) are the result of asking the right questions to establish goals and thinking through the important feelings and behaviour that are to be supported. Good spaces do not force behaviour contrary to goals, such as dependency, or over emphasise unimportant goals, such as tolerance for waiting'. This approach can be found in the work of Prescott, Jones and Kritchevsky back in 1972 (cited in Greenman, Jim 1988).

CHAPTER 3

General planning and design considerations

This chapter covers some of the elements that apply to planning and designing the whole of the outdoor play space. Subsequent chapters will describe how to plan and design specific areas within the playground.

This chapter includes:

3.1 Safety and risk management

Designers need to plan a playground with room for challenge that does not include any blatant risk that could cause major injury. An ongoing informed approach to assessing and eliminating serious risk, based on observation of children at play and on new information as it becomes available, tempered with a healthy appreciation of children's play and need for challenge, is imperative.

There can never be a totally safe playground. However, the pressures to plan out risk are significant. In the UK, ROSPA (the Royal Society for the Prevention of Accidents) warns that: 'Playground managers may be sued for negligence if they fail to take reasonable care to ensure their playgrounds are safe and avoid accidents they could reasonably have foreseen would happen.'

Managing risk may still mean that small injuries are acceptable, and may in fact provide learning opportunities, such as being pricked by a thorn or getting a grazed knee from a fall.

Generous spatial provision which allows for a wide diversity and variety of potential play greatly assists meeting play needs. Minor injuries may occur but often they are not as acute as those in small tight playgrounds where insufficient play is holding back their enjoyment and development of skills.

The funding of new centres must take account of the costs of designing spaces that allow children to meet their developmental needs through play, rather than cutting costs by providing an off-the-shelf 'safe' design.

Figure 3.1 Chapel Hill Community Kindergarten, Brisbane Australia: large smooth boulders are actively sought out by children seeking challenge

Figure 3.2 Chapel Hill Community Kindergarten, Brisbane Australia: discovering the joy of low level branches when seeking challenge

Some planning points to consider in relation to safety are:

▶ Ensure ease of pedestrian and viewing access for both children and staff.
▶ Locate high-risk areas, for example swings and high platforms, away from the main flow of activities, but where they still can be readily viewed and accessed by staff.
▶ Demarcate areas to assist in grouping together compatible activities which can minimise the risk of conflict.
▶ Provide clearly defined access corridors at key points of access within the playground where major traffic occurs, but not at the expense of excluding small getaway hidey spaces.
▶ Provide ample free-fall zones in line with relevant playground standards so that in the event of a child having a vertical fall they will land on a safe impact absorbing surface.
▶ Provide soft fall surface areas to accommodate high level movable equipment or to accommodate movable equipment used in conjunction with play platforms and swings.
▶ Ensure that movable equipment has an appropriate impact absorbing surface (e.g. finely mulched barkchip, to a depth will conform to relevant safety standards of your country) beneath it that conforms to the relevant standards of your country.
▶ Provide ample clearance around movable equipment and incorporate subtle barriers to prevent through-traffic and heighten children's awareness of the risk. Potential solutions include: horizontal tree trunks, low fence, rubber tyre steps up into the area or raised garden beds.
▶ Ensure the swing arc areas extend either side of the swing.
▶ Take account of the effects of excessive sun and heat, and select non-poisonous plants in planting schemes.

3.2 Sustainability

Recognition of the role of sustainability in assisting early childhood education and the important role it plays in caring for the natural environment, lays the foundations for assisting children to develop an appreciation and understanding of environmental limits and the need to organise economies and society accordingly – or what is called 'sustainable development'. Whilst need is acknowledged it is not as readily understood and practiced.

For example, the Australian Children's Education and Care Quality Authority (ACECQA) has a National Quality Standard which states that a centre should 'take an active role in caring for its environment and contribute to a sustainable future' (ACECQA, 2014).

The emergence of sustainability awareness in the last fifteen years (approximately) is already covering a constructive range of approaches extending from the need for 'educational sustainability' (Julie Davis, Australia); that 'play is fundamental to sustainable learning' promoted by Sue Elliott (Australia); the essential word of play in natural settings by Claire Warden in the UK and the practical application of children's play in wild nature settings in the work of Niki Buchan.

Whilst the intent of achieving sustainability in planning for design and implementation particularly during the design stages is less clearly understood in terms of physical environment its role in underpinning effective practices has been less readily conveyed. The reality exists that the level of training in early childhood centres for use of outdoor areas and the state of present government legislation covering physical environment does not provide the support to this excellent child related advance that these document provide. In practice much of the work is blocked by the legacy of tight small spaces by parties without experience in design that is not

Figure 3.3 Enka School, Istanbul, Turkey: sound initial planting creating green sustainability with steep, challenging access sought by children

Figure 3.4 Enka School, Istanbul, Turkey: discovering the joy of playing with seasonal leaves

based on child development or parties who do speak with no experience in planning. In reality much comes from well intentioned sources which are too often commercially driven and create a hindrance to the effective implementation of a physical setting which will expand and develop high levels of teaching.

> Education for sustainability in early childhood education has been validly criticised as being an under examined field.
>
> (Davis, Julie M 2010)

It is essential that the focus be on children's needs and sustainability should underpin the design and development of children's centres, including the outdoor play spaces. This immediately puts demands on greater consideration being given to the outdoor space provided and the spatial provision required for sustainable practices. In practice this means that a party sound knowledge of young children's requirements and design is used to assist those selecting sites and developing the plans for centres. It is vital that the designers work alongside early childhood education experts to ensure the design is first and foremost based on children's needs and developmental requirements remain at the heart of the scheme.

The outdoor play space setting has a vital role to enable children to learn about sustainability. But too often the spaces are unsuitable settings which constrain the support and play teaching practices needed to foster awareness and understanding of sustainable development. When planning an effective outdoor play space, sustainability can be considered in the following ways:

▶ Work with the existing environment and topography, rather than simply clearing the site and imposing a design from scratch.

▶ Check the site and make sure that all the potentially available space is being available e.g. large wide garden beds for visual viewing but blocked from child access.

▶ Enable opportunities for children to interact with, and learn from, the natural environment through, for example, natural play areas and seasonal planting.

▶ Select materials according to low environmental impact, and think about how the centre can minimise carbon-based energy and water use.

▶ Maximise the climatic advantages and protect against the extremes through elements such as shade and seasonal choice of planting.

▶ Identify how children can be involved in the ongoing maintenance and care of the outdoor spaces.

3.3 Entry areas

This is the point where children and adults enter the centre. Some centres will have a secure gate as part of the external fence, and then a walk to the building. Others will have a secure door that leads directly into the entry area. Whatever the arrangement, people arriving need to experience a secure but welcoming entry. Every centre needs to be able to cope with a large flow of children and adults moving safely in and out.

The design should reflect local circumstances and provide a supportive entry to families and the community. In particular the design needs to account for the variety of weather conditions that people will be arriving in. For example, the arrival area needs to be flexible enough to cope with people closing umbrellas or taking off coats. In many communities it is convenient to provide safe storage area for scooters, strollers and bikes (including those for adult carers who may be dropping off by bike).

The welcoming area may have to double as a socialising space, perhaps where parents and carers can stay on and chat. At other times of the day, the entry area may be able to provide a quiet retreat or play area for the children.

For main gates or doors, consider the following:

▶ Make the gates/doors a major focal point of interest: cast iron gates, or solid gates with peep holes for looking out, offer a sense of adventure and anticipation. The height of the gate should be a minimum of 1300mm, possibly more depending on the site, with child-proof latches and a self-closing action. For doors, consider a colour that provides the centre with an identity that reinforces the sense of arrival for children.

▶ Ensure the gates/doors are secure and easily supervised by staff to prevent unauthorised entry or exit while at the same time creating an inviting place for children and their families. Additional security features (such as motion-detection lighting or a secure intercom entry) will be needed in some locations.

▶ Use double gates with childproof latches if this will be the only point of entry for small trucks during maintenance.

▶ Finish the gates off at the same height as the adjoining fence (high fences and gates can be institutional and threatening).

For entry areas consider the following, if appropriate:

▶ Install a wide, hard, non-slip, all-weather path or ramp to assist the use of prams and strollers.

▶ Include storage points adjoining this area for parents who need to leave prams, car seats and bikes during the day.

▶ Include elements that support socialisation for children and waiting adults, such as benches, landscaping within a garden setting and possibly with arches, pergolas or simple seasonal trees. The area needs to be welcoming and inviting because it will introduce the children to the facility and allow them to get oriented.

▶ Ensure that the pathway to the entry area does not create a marked intrusion to the play spaces.

3.4 Ground surfaces

During play children are constantly in contact with the ground surfaces. They provide a wealth of sensory experiences through different textures, types and forms. Surfaces should be selected with care, with choices being governed by sustainability, sensory richness, aesthetics, play needs, maintenance and safety.

As young children are not only curious, but nearer to the ground, they will notice and readily respond to different surface textures, patterns and colours. On warm days, playing barefoot on a variety of surfaces will help children to gain better mastery of their feet. The varied tactile textures, along with the visual changes created by the use of different surfaces, will help heighten a child's perception of where they are in the playground. If these are attractive changes, they can make the area more welcoming and pleasing, providing visual enjoyment and a sense of place which can suggest a certain type of play.

Because of the resourceful nature of children's play, ground surfaces will invariably become a material and surface for play. Children will want to dig and shape earth, pat and smooth sand, shape, rake and cart loose surface materials, draw with chalk on hard surfaces, balance between paving blocks, roll and lie on grass, and hose down hard surfaces. These are all play options, many of them unstructured, and should be allowed as they enhance a child's discovery and resourcefulness during play.

The ongoing viability of most surfaces particularly in tight heavily used playgrounds depends on maintenance. This should be kept in mind when decisions are made regarding selection, siting and application so that loose surface materials can easily be replenished, lawns watered and hard surfaces laid in such a way that they do not crack and can be cleaned easily.

If safety and play options are to be fully realised, the following points need to be considered when selecting and siting ground surfaces:

▶ Type of play intended for each area: is it quiet or busy and risk-taking?
▶ Characteristics of the total site, such as: the slope of the land; is it prone to erosion, frequently damp or in the shade?
▶ Characteristics of individual areas: these will help clarify siting of play areas and the selection of suitable ground surfaces.
▶ Climatic factors affecting surface viability: constant damp will rapidly decompose some materials. In tropical climates rain can wash away loose surface material, causing rapid erosion. In hot, arid climates materials may be constantly hot under foot, while in cold climates some loose impact-absorbing materials, like bark chip, may turn into hard ice.
▶ Cost: this includes both initial outlay and ongoing maintenance costs to ensure that the chosen surfaces do not become a constant financial drain.

3.4.1 Soft fall surfaces

Approximately a third to a quarter of a playground generally needs to be covered with a soft fall surface material. The main areas will be under climbing equipment, swings and any elevated play feature from which a child may fall. The range of potential soft fall surface materials, both natural and man-made, is large. Chosen surfaces should be tested for impact attenuation (that is, its shock absorption properties). However, testing to date has revealed that some traditional surfaces cannot sufficiently minimise the risk of injury. While a lawn of thick, lush grass may provide enough protection from a fall height of 600mm, to maintain grass of this quality in a heavily used early childhood centre is virtually impossible. Soft fall materials, especially in active areas, should be tested to ensure they will provide enough impact attenuation properties to prevent injuries.

Surface material for high-risk potential fall areas of the playground should be selected from materials tested by a certified testing laboratory and laid to the recommended depth. Other points to consider are:

▶ Will the material cut or be a penetration hazard?
▶ Are the particles so large that they will inhibit children playing without shoes on?
▶ Are the particles of a size that cannot be easily inhaled?
▶ Does the material attract an unusual amount of vermin or pests?
▶ Does the material readily cause a high allergic response?
▶ Is the material toxic?
▶ Does it pose a fire hazard?
▶ Is it slippery when wet or dry?
▶ Is it relatively resistant to environmental wear in the climatic areas in which it is being used?
▶ Does it retain heat (like some rubber-based materials) so that it is unbearable to walk on in hot weather?
▶ Will the material freeze into hard particles of ice in a very cold conditions?
▶ If they are materials that will require periodic replenishment, will they always be readily available?

Observing the considerations below will help to minimise the potential for children coming to major injury while playing:

▶ Check impact attenuation properties against relevant local standards, and select a surface according to these. This requires establishing the maximum potential fall height and the capacity of the ground surface to provide an impact absorbing surface that will prevent major injuries. Ensure you obtain written guarantees.
▶ Use an approved granular soft fall surface material laid to a recommended uncompacted depth, and then compacted to a recommended depth (the uncompacted depth is the reference point when trying to establish the quantity of soft fall material needed for an area).
▶ Retain the soft fall surface material within an area in order to maintain its recommended compacted depth. This can be done by using a border or recessing the area into the ground. The edging should be either flush with the adjoining ground surface in a sunken pit area or sited so that there is a marked step between this area and the adjoining space so that children are less likely to trip.
▶ Determine the size of the soft fall surface by the area of potential fall. It should extend a minimum of 2m out from equipment 1.5m high (and preferably a lot further) so that there is ample provision of soft fall surface material under areas where items of movable equipment (for example, trestles, planks, ladders and nets) are used in conjunction with fixed structures. The placement of borders around the area should allow ample clearance, at least 2m from a fixed structure, to prevent a child hitting a hard narrow edge in the event of a fall.
▶ Ensure that the earth base is level and free of any protrusions, for example rocks or roots, so that a uniform depth of soft fall surface material is attained. Failure to retain and place soft fall surface material on a level base has resulted in the entire surface material being either eroded or swept away during heavy rainfall.
▶ Check artificial surfaces (such as rubberised surfaces and artificial grass) for the depth of rubber and impact absorbing materials underneath the grass. All contracts should be checked for the maximum potential fall height above these surfaces. Obtain a written guarantee that the surface meets the required impact absorbing properties.

Off all the soft fall surface materials used finely mulched barkchip when well laid and contained within an area has proved to be one of the most repeatedly utilised surfaces primarily due to its impact absorbing qualities, soft texture and resistance to heat.

3.4.2 Lawn and synthetic artificial grass

Lawn is an ideal natural surface material, which is attractive and pleasant underfoot. While initially relatively inexpensive to lay, it requires a budget to be set for ongoing maintenance. To ensure that it lasts and is well maintained it is important to observe the following:

▶ Do not lay turf in areas of heavy traffic near the building, or in shaded areas, or next to a sandpit without a sweeping edge in between.

▶ When selecting the turf take into account the local climatic conditions so that it will survive heavy use and can be easily maintained. The emphasis should be on maintaining surface cover, not the quality of the turf.

▶ Include a sub-surface watering system to allow for regular watering after children have gone home – this will also prevent play on a wet surface, which will rapidly wear out the lawn. The initial cost will soon be outweighed since the lawn will not have to be constantly re-turfed.

▶ Consider reinforcing lawn with a mat or mesh material in high-use areas. The quality of available products varies: some are permanent and thus will degrade after the lawn is established. Their use can help prevent depression in the lawn, protect the root system and aid drainage of surface water, as well as help retain surfaces, slopes or mounds.

Artificial synthetic grass should be considered when a playground is so small or shady that grass would not survive under constant daily use. Although expensive initially, it is easy to maintain and provides an alternative to bare earth. It is imperative that the total playground surface is not covered with artificial grass to ensure a natural setting for play and learning experiences can occur. Its success in the long term depends on careful selection and installation.

Before deciding on a supplier, check some of their previous projects to ensure that their workmanship is satisfactory. Ask for a guarantee on both the chosen product and their work. When selecting a synthetic grass surface check that the material:

▶ is weather resistant in all types of climates, for example long periods of hot sun or snow, or near salty sea air;

▶ can be easily hosed down;

▶ is stain- and mildew-resistant;

▶ will not track easily and can have spot repairs in the event of accidental damage, such as fire or vandalism;

▶ will not stretch and ripple;

▶ is not too harsh and scratchy underfoot for young children.

Artificial synthetic grass can be laid successfully on a sand base, which is preferable as it allows water to drain though more readily and provides a marginally less hard surface. Check that:

▶ adequate run-off and drainage is provided to prevent future maintenance problems caused by pooling water;

▶ the details for fixing the edges of the material are sound, and make sure they are flush with the adjoining material to enable easy access by children and limit the risk of tripping.

3.4.3 Hard surfaces

When sited and laid with care, hard surfaces can provide an attractive variation in heavy-use, low-risk areas of a playground that need easy maintenance. These surfaces are best sited in busy areas such as the outdoor play hub, around sandpit edges, paths, terraces, and terrace extensions and wading pools, but never in active or open areas. In other less trafficked, quiet areas compacted earth surfaces will suffice. When selecting surfaces consider the following:

▶ Use patterned paving or brickwork in preference to concrete and asphalt. This can be laid in a number of different ways (in circular, basket-weave, herringbone or other patterns) and will create a more attractive, stimulating environment.

▶ Lay bricks and paving blocks on a flat surface with a very slight fall to deflect surface water. Place them on a concrete slab or plastic sheeting and bedding sand then infill with a sand and concrete dry mix.

▶ Lay paving bricks, tiles and concrete on a well compacted base so that sinkage, which creates cracked uneven surfaces, and water pooling does not occur.

▶ Avoid sharp contrasts in colour between tiles as it can cause a distraction to play. A more adaptable solution is one with a subtle combination of colours so the mood of the space can change according to season and forms of usage to inspire further levels of play.

▶ Use slip resistant surfaces and ensure that they are smooth and even to avoid grazing and tripping.

▶ Consider aggregate or other surface materials, if not too rough and hard, as an inexpensive solution in low-risk areas of the playground.

3.5 Drainage

Poor drainage, particularly in heavy rainfall areas, can cause excessive maintenance and lead to major interruptions to the use of the playground. Top soil, sand and loose surface material can easily wash away, exposing rough surfaces and blocking drains. Entry to centres can be obstructed and use of equipment limited because of pooling water, and lawns can be rapidly destroyed by the combination of traffic flow and surface water. Lack of planning to cope with heavy downpours and subsequent drain-off all too often results in buildings and sheds being flooded. Paradoxically, surface water, if controlled and used effectively, can be a valuable play material for children. Seek professional advice on drainage to prevent it becoming a recurring problem.

Natural drainage is the best solution, but this is rarely achievable, particularly after building and playground development has been carried out without an overall appraisal of the problem. Often the siting of the building and placement of sheds and mounds can cause problems. The following methods have been used with success in a range of early childhood services:

▶ Flat and sunken land can be filled and agricultural pipes can be set under the ground.

▶ Water can be deflected by strategically placing small mounds, mounded garden beds, boulders and horizontal logs near fences – however, these solutions cannot be used in spaces where they will hinder access, traffic flow or play.

▶ Shallow swale drains can be linked to a storm water system.

▶ On sloping sites, terracing compatible to child use can deflect water – use boulders, horizontal logs or rubber tires filled with soil.

▶ Small, undrained areas can be planted heavily with moisture absorbing plants.

▶ Sub-surface drainage may require a network of sunken agricultural pipes.

Severe drainage problems may need to be dealt with in a more structural manner:

▶ In heavy rainfall areas a grated drain along the edge of the verandah to the building is essential when the playground slopes down toward the building. Ensure that the grating is too heavy for a child to lift.

▶ At the lowest part of the playground a large gully can be set into the ground and linked to a stormwater system. To be effective it is essential that solid metal grids are installed for safety reasons, although ensure that there is a flat metal surface that children can walk on without catching their toes.

▶ In upper areas of a playground the provision of a shallow swale drain to a level change between different sections of the playground produces a watercourse, which can create hours of delight.

3.6 Planting

Varied planting is critical to establishing a sensory rich play space which will aid children's perception of sustainability. Children will see colour, movement and variety in the shapes of leaves and flowers. They will watch plants grow and leaves fall and seeds, flowers, leaves and fruit develop. They will smell herbs, the perfume of flowers, newly mown grass and natural mulch after rain and feel the bark on trees, the softness of petals, or crush dry leaves in their hands. They can hear the rustle of leaves, the crunch underfoot of dry mulch, the rattle of seeds in pods or enjoy the taste of fruit, vegetables and herbs.

From a planning perspective it is vital to use a small multidisciplinary team incorporating either an arborist, horticulturist or landscape architect. The foundation for any planning should be to listen to feedback from an experienced early childhood practitioner and, preferably, observation of children's play at the proposed or another site to increase the depth of understanding.

Careful assessment of existing plants within a playground space needs to be carried out to ensure that they are viable in the long-term and that they will be suitable within the context of a well-planned playground. Ask questions such as, do the plants provide shade, or are they located in a section of the play area where they will be a hazard to children? The master-plan should maximise the potential of existing vegetation and ensure that it will be protected during construction.

New plants should not impede easy supervision of children even when they are in an area they regard as 'hidden', for example inside their mock cubby house within a shrub.

3.6.1 Design considerations

Consider the following:

- ▶ Plant a wide variety of varying textures (trees, shrubs, vines, low-level plants such as ground covers, vegetable gardens) to create a beautiful as well as functional playground.
- ▶ Plant to create a three-dimensional space.
- ▶ Define spaces between play areas using plants, particularly if they are lower than adult eye level to aid supervision, without interrupting the children's play.
- ▶ Consider planting free-form flowing garden beds to create large and small quiet areas and secret places.
- ▶ Enhance under-utilised spaces at the edges of sheds, adjoining fence lines, or at either side of steps by planting – anything from raised herb garden beds to a cluster of hardy ferns or grasses.
- ▶ Use vines to soften spaces, create shade and enhance a sense of enclosure.
- ▶ Avoid planting trees where excessive shade may result in lawns failing to grow and where their roots will cause problems with service lines and buildings.
- ▶ When incorporating trees always consider the long-term implications of tree roots, particularly in small playgrounds where protruding tree roots can create major trip hazards – in contrast, tree roots in larger playgrounds can be a wonderful area to climb around and to create a private space.

When selecting plants bear in mind the following:

- ▶ Choose a wide variety of plants (such as vines, ferns, cacti, shrubs and flowering annuals) as each can provide a different sensory experience.
- ▶ Choose some mature plants for early effect.
- ▶ Make sure that the majority of plants are robust and easy to handle.
- ▶ Provide a variety of flowering plants for children to pick.
- ▶ Plant showy seasonal indicators, for example spring blossoms or bright autumn leaves.
- ▶ Plant to attract birds and other wildlife.
- ▶ Plant herbs, flowers and leaves that stimulate the sense of smell.
- ▶ Provide as many textures as possible (different barks, leaves, stems and trunks).
- ▶ Provide plants that children can see grow and taste such as fruiting trees, vegetables, vines, shrubs and ground covers.
- ▶ Plant trees that have leaves that rustle or are deciduous so that children can crunch leaves underfoot.
- ▶ Plant a variety of colours to aid the children's recognition of colours.
- ▶ Provide plants that are indigenous to the area: this can aid maintenance and show children the difference between native and imported varieties.

▶ Plant big, deciduous trees for winter sun and summer shade.

▶ Plant spreading shrubs that can be pruned underneath to create quiet nooks.

▶ Plant trees that can carry ropes and have boughs that are low enough for children to climb on with ease.

▶ Do not select plants that are poisonous to touch or eat.

3.6.2 Soil

Check soil type with a horticulturist to find the best way of preparing the soil and for helping to select plants. Alternatively, a parent or grandparent may be willing and able to give advice on local conditions, what grows in the area and availability.

The compaction of soil in the total area will vary from place to place. During construction, building rubbish is often dumped and then covered over with good topsoil. Compacted or polluted soil will not let plants grow to their potential so the soil needs to be loosened up to let the plant roots spread out and any pollution removed before planting occurs.

Before a site is chosen, previous uses need to be investigated to check that the soil is not contaminated and is safe for young, growing bodies to play on. Any soil or other material that is imported onto the site also needs to be cleaned of any contamination.

3.7 Fencing

The selection of fencing should be related to function – not all fences will need to be the same. Just as much attention should be paid to the internal fences as to the external (or boundary) fences. They should combine functional effectiveness with subtle invitational and play-rich elements. For example, careful design of boundary fences can provide security while also mitigating traffic or noise pollution. They can also add to the attractiveness of the centre and provide play opportunities that allow for 'views to beyond'.

Boundary fences must be childproof and constructed in such a way that children cannot climb over them. Fences should be chosen so that they do not present a foothold. The height of fences can be as low as 1.3m if there is an attractive but safe view, and up to 1.5m depending on the adjoining land uses. This can vary markedly due to differing government licensing requirements. Note that noise from the street or from neighbours can dictate the choice of a core sound-resistant fence made of concrete block, brick or compressed fibre-board sheeting. Higher fence lines may be required for centres located on busy roads or on corner sites.

The practice of using internal fencing within a playground has both advantages and constraints depending on the needs of children and function of the division. The most common use directly relates to age and skill variations in children. Small toddlers and babies often find competing with older more agile children in a bigger playground threatening. However, children in the transition years may need to move between the older/younger areas in accordance with their developmental level or play interest – this can be overcome by careful design. Avoid fencing off different sections of a playground as this inhibits important social contact and development between children of different ages.

Access between playground sections is important. Double gates may be required for maintenance purposes, but can also be used to free-up child access at the teacher's discretion. A sign of a child's expanding skill range is the pushing of a block or a chair against a low internal fence in an attempt to climb. It is then time to celebrate this child's new sense of empowerment, open the gates and accompany her/him on visits to the playground for older children.

For boundary fences consider the following:

▶ Ensure that they are structurally sound and give consideration to materials that are easy and relatively inexpensive to maintain.

▶ If solid fences are essential for safety reasons, consider cutting peepholes at child height or use see-through panels, especially if there is an attractive view beyond the centre.

▶ Think about the climate: solid fences can block unpleasant winds in colder climates and provide a welcome heat trap in winter – in hotter climates, more porous fencing such as vertical slats or pool-safe fences with or without bamboo or brush panels for seasonal use allow in cooling breezes.

▶ Add vegetation to the fencing: this might include vines growing along stainless steel wires on brackets 150mm above the top of a fence (to prevent a foot-hold).

▶ Create interest and stimulation for children by attaching varied play panels to portions of walls or fences such as wind chimes, murals, drawings boards and so on.

If internal fences are used consider the following:

▶ Use low level, vertical slat fences (that do not provide a foothold) 600mm high for toddlers to pull themselves up and view into an adjoining playground.

▶ Provide a low, flat bench on the top of the vertical slat fence approximately 200 to 300mm wide to act as an upright play surface – a bench can also be used as a division in a sandpit with one end of the sandpit being designated for the younger children.

▶ Install raised garden beds with flowers and plants at a height of 500mm to provide a surface for a crawling child to pull themselves up into an upright position to provide support as they learn to walk while enabling them to view out to the adjoining playground beyond.

▶ Use panel fences of varying shapes and types with Perspex viewing panels and sensory panels, to invite use on both sides, for example running sticks over bamboo, different tones when beaten, peephole windows of different colours.

3.8 Services

3.8.1 Water supply

The inclusion and placement of water supply systems needs to be considered carefully. For example, the siting of a watercourse should enable the water used for play purposes to extend to watering and nurturing of the garden areas to a level that this becomes part of expanding children's understanding of how to create and sustain a manageable environment.

Water is used for play, maintenance of gardens or lawns and for cleaning up after messy play. The source of water is typically urban reticulation, but in drier climates it tends to be supplemented by on-site storage structures (which must be sited to avoid supervisory issues). In terms of outlets, a minimum of three taps will be needed in a small playground and about six in larger areas. Site taps beside play areas that rely on water – such as messy play areas – and storage areas for ease of cleaning before putting items away. Some facilities choose sophisticated automatic lawn/garden watering systems, but this is in addition to water needed in sandpits, for watercourses, wading pools, child gardens, cleaning equipment and so on.

3.8.2 Electricity supply

Not every facility will need electricity outlets within the playground. However, consider situations with daily needs such as ventilation/light in storage sheds, light/music within a gazebo and security lighting. Shelves on a verandah at a height of at least 1.5m with a power point have proved to be heavily used in many centres for music and night time access for meetings or special occasions. There may also be periodic social events (such as productions in an amphitheatre) which will be easier to manage if there is an adjacent electricity outlet.

Be aware of the need for child-proofing such outlets and the threat of vandalism, particularly in high-density urban spaces. In these areas centres will benefit from external lights to minimise vandalism risks.

3.9 Maintenance

Maintenance of the physical environment is vital to ensure the long-term viability of any outdoor play space. Poor maintenance can inhibit the purpose of the playground, especially when it limits and inhibits children carrying out their play ideas.

Effective planning and implementation of a playground underpins how easy it will be to maintain. This is particularly important when establishing new centres where siting and allocation of the spatial area, drainage provision and some basic early earthworks are usually required. But it matters for minor additions in existing play spaces too, such as preparing for a new sandpit; in others, considering maintenance implications at the planning stage may ensure the difference between a viable child accessible playground or not. Cost cutting during the planning stage in practice proves to be far more expensive in the long-term.

At its most damaging, poor maintenance can cause unnecessary injuries to children, such as falls due to a rope breaking, and cuts from sharp edges, protruding nails and bolts, and rusting equipment that buckles under a child's weight.

A good playground can be ruined by a lack of regular maintenance, which often means failing to attend to small problems that become bigger over time, with detrimental impacts on cost. Allocating a budget for ongoing maintenance is just as important for the playground as it is for the early childhood centre building and equipment. The number of hours during which the playground is used can be calculated to arrive at a daily or yearly figure – multiplying this by the number of children can indicate the areas of heavy usage and establish the probable amount of wear and tear. In a well-planned and set out playground daily wear and tear can be viewed as a mark of success and a clear indication that the play spaces have inspired children so much that they use them constantly. Smaller playgrounds typically have more intense use and will require a higher level of constant maintenance.

Vandalism is also a problem in many centres. There is no easy solution to these problems and each needs to be looked at separately. Designers can help by creating playgrounds that are inexpensive and easy to maintain. Neighbours can be enlisted to keep a watchful eye out for vandals and be supplied with a contact telephone number for emergencies. Moveable equipment can be stored each night in a lock-up shed (refer to 8.5 Storage sheds, page 92). These precautions will remove some of the temptation, although not all, for vandals.

The task of providing a well-maintained playground belongs to several parties. Successful implementation depends on clear and open communication between all parties. Set up an ongoing maintenance system that will survive changes in personnel, and that is designed to achieve a safe play environment, uncompromised by the need for easy maintenance.

3.9.1 Maintenance tasks to consider when planning a playground

The initial planning of a playground should aim to reduce maintenance to a minimum to avoid unnecessary ongoing costs and to facilitate maintenance. Points to consider include:

▶ Regular plant care: all large trees should be regularly checked by an experienced arborist to assist with the removal of any dead wood and to check the condition of the tree to assess its long-term viability; removal of shade canopies can have a disastrous effect on the cool shade provision in hot climates.
▶ Access for trucks: this is to enable sand to be delivered right to the sandpit, top soil and new turf onto the lawn, sandy loam to the digging pit and bark chip and other soft fall surface material besides climbing equipment, thus avoiding unnecessary labour and cost.
▶ Drainage of ground surface water: it is vital that most of the playground clears rapidly after rain so children can avoid using damp surfaces with ensuing wear and tear on surfaces such as lawns.
▶ Siting of drainage traps and gullies: these should be along the edges of terraces, and be open-grated drains with grates that can be readily removed by an adult for maintenance.

▶ Siting taps in strategic places whilst being critical for assisting play can also ease the task of watering lawns and gardens and hosing down paved areas.

▶ Fitting taps with automatic timers: these can be left on after the children have gone home. This is particularly important in day-care centres that have long contact hours with children. Also consider sub-surface watering systems as the initial financial outlay is often recouped through reduced ongoing maintenance costs.

▶ Selection of ground surfaces: consider the climatic, local and shade needs of the playground, ensuring that lawns are not completely shaded, and heavily used areas have surfaces to match use.

▶ Retain edges around loose surface material areas: this will assist with the retention of materials particularly in tight, small playgrounds. Wide sweeping edges assist this maintenance and also provide heavily utilised play surfaces which extend play. The edging should be flush with the adjoining surface to prevent children tripping over it, and to facilitate mowing of adjoining lawns. Edgings like these can minimise unnecessary intermingling of surface materials, which is important if loose surface materials are going to retain their depth and impact absorbing qualities.

▶ Site lawns in open sunny positions to ensure their survival, and select turf that is robust enough to survive almost constant use and is suited to the climatic and soil needs of the area.

▶ Avoid higher maintenance costs by designing out water pooling even on areas intended as flat surfaces whether for paving or as open lawn.

▶ Ensure sandpits have wide sweeping edges that have a slight fall into the pit as this will aid sweeping and hosing sand back into the pit. Boulders and high timber edges can inhibit this.

▶ Plan to install equipment that is easier to maintain: standardised fittings are cheaper and easier to refurbish, and re-staining timber equipment easier than recoating with paint.

▶ Site plants in areas that minimise constant pruning, and choose species that are hardy and easy to look after. Include ground covers to reduce the need for constant weeding, and indigenous plants, or plants suited to the area.

CHAPTER 4

Natural play areas

4.1 Why children need natural play areas

The language of 'educating for sustainability' is relatively modern however, the value of children's contact with nature has been built into good outdoor playground design for decades. Children's centres have an important role to introduce children to the idea of caring for their environment, and natural play areas provide an ideal setting. This chapter refers to 'natural play areas' as a loose description for a range of outdoor play elements that encourage contact with nature: water features, digging patches, gardens and animal and bird homes.

Play involving these elements is characteristically messy. Young children may begin this process as a form of sensory enquiry which evolves into exploring a wider range of places and materials within the playground. Older children of 4–5 years will welcome the opportunity to be physically creating, and acting out fantasies and ideas on a scale which is nearer to the real thing. Such activity will also aid a child's perception and understanding of those elements in daily life that they find exciting but difficult to fully comprehend. This results in a sustained level of interest as they build innumerable mud pies and often complex dams, watercourses, bridges, road systems and islands.

Katharine Whitehorn reminds us that, 'richness of experience, not tidy perfection, is the aim of the whole thing.' [cited in Lady Allen of Hurtwood 1968]

Children's cognitive learning is aided by this play. As they get older they begin to perceive how variations in one element of their play affect another element; for example how much soil to use

Figure 4.1 Chapel Hill Community Kindergarten, Brisbane Australia: the joy of observation from a height after the challenge of climbing

Figure 4.2 Chapel Hill Community Kindergarten, Brisbane Australia: children observe others to establish the best way to take on a new challenge involving a degree of risk

and how best to move it to make a dam wall, then how long to run the tap in order to fill the dam. This learning may be expanded further, enabling children to turn their attention to another section of their play and return when the dam is almost full. These cognitive skills are often acquired through trial and error during intense periods of play demanding gross muscular skills such as those used by the workman with whom they may be identifying. The actions of shovelling, digging, channelling, hauling, carting, pulling, lifting and pushing, as well as the quieter activities of smoothing, patting, shaping and moulding, heighten children's awareness of the feel, touch and smell of the earth, water and often leaves that are the raw play materials.

Often this play can be solitary, not always because the child lacks social skills, but because of the need to work through a concept and feel the lay of the land before sharing. Most of the time this play appeals to and challenges older children, the 4- to 5-year-olds, who play in unison in small and large groups. Sharing labour to meet a common creative goal will demand and draw out new levels of cooperative play. It may produce leadership within the group not seen elsewhere in the playground, and verbal exchange with command, as well as expression of ideas, fantasies and thoughts.

Digging patches produce work/play which can make a child identify with being older and more responsible, as they dig with spades, build with bits of wood, brick, plastic piping, or use hoses in conjunction with soil and water. Often this play releases tension as children enjoy a legitimate opportunity to construct, destroy and construct again.

Figure 4.3 Chapel Hill Community Kindergarten, Brisbane Australia: after the climb enjoying the quiet retreat to observe others at play

Not only is this kind of messy play fun and necessary developmentally, it can also help children to enjoy better physical health. A growing number of research findings have recommended that children should play with dirt and mud as a way to boost their immune system because it exposes them early to naturally occurring microbes in soil (for example, see Lee 2012).

> Flexibility – to explain children's play or interactions with nature, the common thread is that children can follow their interests and explore the properties of whatever is available to them in their outdoor space.
>
> (Nicki Buchan 2015)

4.2 Water play

Water is a favourite play material of even very young children. Whether used on its own or with other materials water has such potential: it provides endless hours of fascinating and satisfying creative play for young children as they touch, feel, drink, splash and spray it, or contain it by pouring, damming and sponging, or move it by hosing, draining, bucketing and collecting. It is the open-ended nature of water that allows it to be adapted to fit in with any amount of ideas and construction.

Good planning can expand the potential of water play on a larger scale by providing wading pools, watercourses and small ponds.

Figure 4.4 Heavy subtropical planting has created a cooling space where there is a cave to hide in and a shallow water creek

4.2.1 Wading pools and design considerations

As the name implies, children cannot immerse themselves in a wading pool – instead it is an area in which they can walk, sit, pour and splash water, and gain relief from heat. In the colder months a well-designed wading pool can be used empty as a defined place of play, especially when loose parts such as mats, pebbles and puzzles or painting easels etc. are added.

The following guidelines on design details and safety elements need to be considered.

Location

▶ Site the wading pool where water is available (for example, near a tap) and where it can be supervised. Provided these criteria are met then the location can vary according to the size of the site and the placement of adjoining facilities.
▶ Consider siting the wading pool between two specific play areas to provide a natural transition, for example between a nature area and a quiet space. To extend play, a watercourse can lead into the wading pool and allow for drainage through to an adjoining garden bed or drainage system.
▶ Where possible, exploit the available natural materials already within the play space: a small section of embankment, a boulder placed on top of a mound with a tap on the top or changing levels between a given space.
▶ Alternatively, construct the pool on top of a low mound with the watercourse running away from the wading pool down into the digging patch area.

Size, shape and depth

▶ Ensure the wading pool is big enough so that a group of children can use it at the same time. A 3–4m² size is adequate for a small animated group at play, but the final size will depend on the space in the centre and the number of children to be accommodated. It may be designed as a series of interconnected shallow pools, each catering for as many as five or six children. In a very large centre with plenty of space the sound inclusion is a series of interconnected shallow wading pools which creates an excellent break-up of space and allows for a diversity of different forms of play to occur.

▶ Consider installing slightly interconnected changes in level: anything from 150 to 200mm and up to 500mm so children can walk or climb from one level down to another and have the sheer pleasure of walking uphill against a tiered watercourse linking down to a wading pool. The depth should be no more than 150mm.

Surfaces and edges

▶ Use surfaces that are non-slippery, for example rough finished concrete or a more attractive solution of patterned brickwork.

▶ Consider making edges flush with ground level for easy access and to prevent tripping, or construct wide raised edges approximately 300mm high that a child can sit on safely and which will still enable easy access. Boulder or timber steps will also create an enjoyable means of access.

▶ Ensure that if the edges are constructed from timber they will not readily rot, splinter or attract white ants.

Water and drainage

▶ Install at least one tap immediately adjoining the pool to allow for easy access to the water by both adults and children.

▶ Install simple systems that drain rapidly so that water is not left in the pool when it is unsupervised. This must occur at least daily for both health and safety reasons. The pool water can be drained away through a link to a storm water system or into a digging patch or adjoining garden bed.

▶ Install a sunken drain outlet with a small grated cover over a base of the pool using a 50–60mm bath plug to retain water. Make provision for a silt trap designed for easy removal of sand by adults or children. This prevents blockage of drains, especially when drained over a distance.

Shade

▶ Consider siting the wading pool under large deciduous trees for winter sun and summer shade – if they are deciduous some extra maintenance will be required to prevent rotting leaves from creating slippery surfaces, a task children often enjoy.

▶ Use artificial shade cover year round or for the hot summer months. Permanent sails need to be carefully placed to make sure that they provide maximum shade during the hottest and most heavily utilised times in the playground.

▶ Consider a fixed roof shelter or pergola with vines to offer seasonal variations or permanent shade throughout the year. In tropical climates fixed roof shelters need to almost be a mandatory requirement for shade provision.

4.2.2 Watercourses or creeks and design considerations

Less structured watercourses and creeks are popular with children because they provide them with room to build and create, to make their own rivers, dams and waterfalls, and to experiment with levels, flows and objects that float. Pay attention to the following considerations:

▶ Locate watercourses away from the main traffic flow areas, ideally adjacent to an active area, and often leading to the digging patch or wading pool.

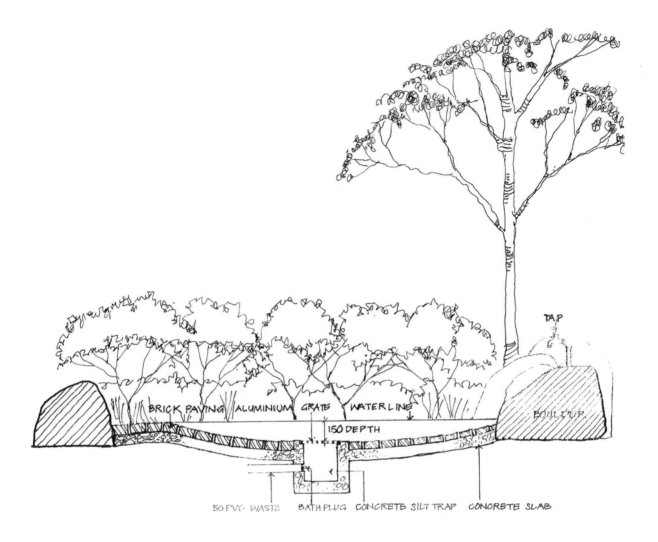

Figure 4.5 A shallow wading pool with a tap, easy drainage and a depth that allows for shallow water play without the risk of drowning on hot days

▶ Keep watercourses shallow (no more than 10–20mm deep for small flows of water).
▶ Consider piping watercourses underground to emerge in another area, which is ideal when traffic flow would be impeded by the watercourse, or a narrow area needs to be traversed.
▶ Let the water flow into the digging pit or garden area, as long as the stream can be controlled and is not excessive, or link to stormwater drains and street gutters.
▶ Use structured watercourses to remove surface water or to move it from one area of play to another.
▶ In small, tight play spaces, create a waterway as a small narrow concrete pathway with items such as pebbles and the use of sluice gates, combined with a tap at the source especially when linked to a digging patch.
▶ In larger play spaces design the watercourse as a more loosely structured element that can also assist with drainage.

4.2.3 Small ponds and design considerations

These can be very versatile. They may be used for keeping guppies, fish, ducks, planting water lilies or simply for children to reflect on and enjoy. When designing a pond, keep safety in mind: a toddler can drown in 5mm of water so it is essential that the pond is sited in a constantly supervised area or has a fixed grated mesh cover.

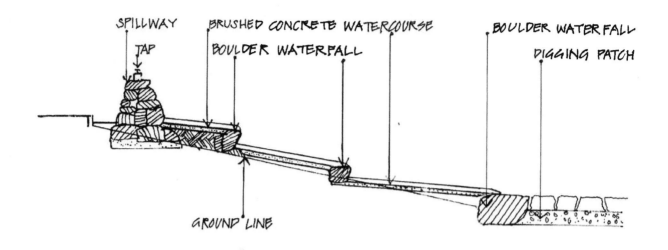

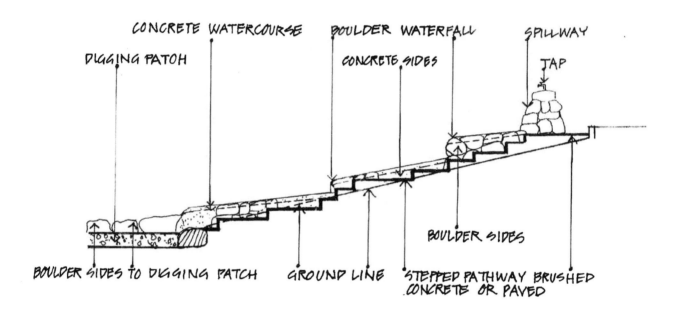

Figure 4.6 The heavily utilised watercourse area is linked to a digging patch: stepped, child-accessible creek and water flow leads down to a digging area

Consider the following when designing a pond.

▶ Choose a shaded part of the quiet area, or a separate secret place that is no more than 2m², with a depth of approximately 250mm (the pool can be above or below ground level).

▶ Use concrete or 10–15mm diameter pebbles on the base of the pool, and use planting in and around the area to create an atmosphere of tranquillity.

▶ Raise the edge of the pond using rounded smooth boulders to a height of up to 500mm – this will provide enough height to stop children running into the pond while allowing them to reach in and view its contents.

▶ Place a piece of cut-to-size reinforcing mesh just below water level to prevent children immersing themselves in the water.

4.3 Children's gardens

Although a planting or gardening programme for children can be carried out throughout most of the playground, there is still a need for setting aside a special area for children to plan, tend and enjoy, which is largely their responsibility to care for and look after. With the support and interest of the teacher they will learn how to plant seeds, bulbs, seedlings and cuttings, and how to water, fertilise, weed and tend the garden. They will learn how to aerate soil, and that earthworms are found in rich soil. They will discover which insects are pests and which plants need sun and more water. They can enjoy the results of these activities as they pick, smell, taste and visually enjoy the developing plants. They can experience different flowering root systems, leaf shapes and colours, and incorporate the products of the garden into activities such as sorting, matching, arranging, cooking and making collages.

4.3.1 Design considerations

The garden should be adjacent to the quiet area or to a small area of unused land. It need not be very large as it is in addition to the existing garden. Consider the following:

▶ Create access on all sides of the garden bed to enable children to tend plants easily.
▶ Use curved or square shapes for larger beds, with pathways of paving blocks, log rounds or compacted earth to facilitate access.
▶ Use narrow garden beds no more than 500–600mm wide adjoining a fence line to accommodate vines and varied planting.
▶ Use raised garden beds or window boxes to enable children to enjoy the garden even while indoors, and so that children in wheelchairs can enjoy tending and viewing the garden.
▶ Provide full and part shaded areas to enable children to experience shade-tolerant plants.
▶ Place a tap or hose close by for easy watering.

4.4 Digging patches

A large unstructured digging patch will provide children with a unique opportunity to create, experiment and develop ideas on a grand scale. With sandy loam soil, and often water as well, they have the opportunity to use two unstructured play materials. This allows their play to have a marked impact on their immediate environment as they build, dismantle and develop ideas which increase in complexity as play proceeds. It is these characteristics that make a digging patch one of the most popular and heavily used areas with the most focused and concentrated play.

The success of a digging patch depends on several factors such as its size, access to water (especially in hot months), the level and type of the surface and the willingness of teachers (and carers) to see that this is an area with rich potential for play learning.

4.4.1 Design considerations

Siting and size

▶ Locate the patch at a far end of the playground, ideally in a slightly sunken area where water can overflow into the space.
▶ Choose a freeform shape, not rectangular boxes as they can constrain play.
▶ Select a space that is a minimum of 10m^2, and ideally more like 25–30m^2.
▶ Design the edges of the digging patch area to be less formal and structured than those used for a sandpit.

Material

▶ Provide loosely packed soil so that children can dig deep with relative ease.
▶ Select the soil base carefully: clay soils that cake hard will frustrate children, damage clothes and present maintenance problems. Use a sandy loam that does not stain clothes, or a mixture of the natural playground surface and sand.

Figure 4.7 Alderley Kindergarten, Brisbane Australia: digging patch with messy, absorbed, continuous shared and imaginative play stimulated after heavy rainfall

Water

► Install a tap at the highest point of the digging patch to create a flow of water.
► Install a smooth boulder cairn with a tap on top.
► Alternatively, utilise a waterfall or natural watercourse leading to, or as part of, the digging patch, which also gives children the opportunity to float objects and create rivers and dams.
► In dry climates, link rainwater tanks directly to the digging patch or to a watercourse that feeds the digging patch. Place rainwater tanks where children can observe them and learn to assess the amount of water that is currently available.

Drainage

► Use excess water flow from the digging patch to water plants throughout the playground.
► Provide underground drainage if necessary on tight sites, and link to the stormwater system or street gutters.
► Seek permission to drain water into a neighbour's garden.

The following design features will add to the natural feel of the area:

► Heavy planting can create an imaginary jungle area with shade. Shade-tolerant plants such as hardy ferns, some native grasses, vines on adjacent fences, deciduous trees or low shrubs to define the area make an exciting play space.
► Small mounds of 500–700mm in a flowing configuration that children can run over create good barriers to retain sandy soil and water.
► Large smooth boulders, horizontal logs or rubber tyres packed with soil create steps and can help retain sandy soil and water.

These open-ended play spaces can be complemented with the extensive use of loose parts including:

► small metal shovels with rounded bases;
► buckets;
► wheelbarrows;
► hand trowels;
► log rounds and medium size boulders (approximately 300mm) which children can shift around and use to shape the surface material, or sit and climb on;
► a recycled table with legs cut down to make a low bench that can be used for piling the surface material, creating elevated watercourses;
► a pulley suspended from a high tree with a knot in it so that it can be pulled out and used for carting buckets and moving in between different areas;
► converted PVC pipes/rain gutters cut into modules and blocks of 500mm or less with standard plumbing joining pieces to create a watercourse by slicing the pipes lengthwise, bevelling the edges and letting the children connect them with a range of different fittings for example Y-bends or S-bends.

4.5 Animals, birds and insects

A well-planned natural playground may invite bird and insect life and provide opportunities for many spontaneous learning experiences. An outdoor play environment can also provide more formal opportunities for children to have contact with animals and birds.

First-hand experience of handling, seeing and tending creatures excites and fascinates young children, allaying their fears, and developing in them a respect, pleasure and awareness of all creatures. Through caring for small creatures children learn about their needs and develop a sense of responsibility by providing them with food, water and protection from the weather. There is sensory pleasure in handling and stroking some animals and a quiet shared relationship in caring for them. This requires children to learn new physical skills so that they can handle creatures with care and respect.

Figure 4.8 Brisbane Australia: child absorbed with sensory exploration and observation of a butterfly

This first-hand experience extends children intellectually as they begin to understand the different classifications and behaviour of animals and develop a concept of animals' life cycles from watching nesting birds, tadpoles turning into frogs or baby guinea-pigs suckling. It may also give them a preliminary understanding of birth and death. Obviously any creature that could be dangerous must be excluded and children will learn why this is so.

These learning experiences are the right of all children and they become particularly important if the home environment is unable to provide it for them. Urban children living in high-rise flats or tight, tidy suburban blocks have particular need of such experiences.

The practicalities – including any health and environmental limitations – must be carefully ascertained by the teacher. Check local council laws, health and fisheries and wildlife regulations to find out if there are any restrictions on keeping certain animals. Children with allergies will also require consideration. Constant maintenance is essential to minimise the risk of disease.

Parts of the quiet area are ideally suited to more planned nature experiences as they are away from boisterous activities that may frighten animals and distract children.

4.5.1 Ideas for incorporating animals and birds into outdoor play spaces

Looking after animals at the centre can provide an excellent focus for teaching and learning about sustainability and sustainable practices. The ideas for including animals and so on are endless, but will depend largely on the viability of the location of the centre and ensuring that the spatial provision for animals does not compromise the diversity of other play options. The following list of suggestions may aid planning, once the amount of land available and the needs of children in a particular facility have been taken into account:

▶ trees, shrubs and vines should always be dominant;
▶ raised bird bath and feeding tables: place at a height of approximately 700mm and position where children can reach them easily to add feed. Siting them in a quiet secret space would be ideal;

Figure 4.9 Child quietly observing a duck's habits and movements

Figure 4.10 Lambs to feed on a cold day stimulating care, respect and understanding of animals

- ▶ small ponds (see Section 4.2.3 on page 45);
- ▶ fixed cages: these are suitable for birds and animals and large enough for children to enter so they can help care for the creatures;
- ▶ hen houses: the choice will depend on the availability of materials and local climatic conditions;
- ▶ movable pet equipment: this could include a portable pet hatch, bird feeder (suspended from a tree so that cats cannot get to the birds), a nectar feeder placed on top of a post (approximately 700mm high), a reptile aquarium, or a portable mouse cage.

Figure 4.11 Discovering that quiet, gentle and slow movements will result in a Kookaburra and other birds staying in the garden to be fed with seeds or observed for longer periods

CHAPTER 5

Quiet play areas

5.1 Why children need quiet play areas

It is necessary to provide spaces to encourage quiet play as this stimulates and encourages the type of play that assists with the development of deep concentration for children as they become absorbed in trying out new ideas and forms of play. Cognitive skills (such as memory, sequencing and representation) are sharpened as a child recalls in increasing detail, imitates, plays, acts out or tries out what they have seen in order to come to terms with it. These thought processes act as a catalyst for developing finer motor skills and increasing mastery of repetitive skills.

Quiet play spaces should enable play as varied as picking flowers, gentle gardening, lying down and looking at trees, sharing time with best friends, building sandcastles and watercourses, connecting pipes to water and learning about drainage, creating art in many and varied forms, dressing up, putting on impromptu concerts and building cubby houses. Quiet areas need to offer a framework where loose parts can readily be added allowing children to shape and extend a wide variety and depth of play (see Chapter 8).

Quiet areas set aside for this kind of play provide space which, by its very size and nature, encourages socialisation and language skills. A large hub or smaller quiet spaces capable of coping with either large or small groups of children are needed. Sandpits are one of the most heavily used of these facilities, especially when they are sited in a sensory rich area. Secret places encourage solitude, quiet thinking and close one-to-one contact. As Jim Greenman puts it:

> Where is there to go to be alone or with a trusted friend or fellow temporary outcast? Quiet spaces scaled to child size – grottoes, nests, perches, miniature picnic tables off a beaten path – all provide wayside rests.

(Jim Greenman 1988)

Provision of such areas should help a child listen, observe, absorb and converse with other children and with the teachers. Quiet play areas help children develop sustained concentration, become creative and socially adept adults of the future.

The term 'quiet area', when viewed in light of children's play, is more apt than the more commonly used landscape term 'passive area', as this play is far from passive in nature. Quiet play spaces are often created by the subtle design of break-up of spaces and form to a level which will trigger children's imagination and allow them to fantasise. To aid concentration the potential for possible interruptions must be minimised. The size, shape and scale of these spaces – a calm semi-enclosure, cosy spaces for one to two children or the provision of a larger defined space for group activities – will suggest the kind of activity but not dictate it. The quiet areas should be approximately a quarter to a third of the total playground.

Quiet areas should be visually attractive. They must be sensory rich and spatially varied, offering a natural progression and flow of space through a variety of uniquely defined areas.

Above all, the aim in designing a quiet area should be to create a flexible space, a stage or setting into which play components, that can be readily adapted by children or teachers to provide an increasing level of complexity, can be incorporated on a daily basis.

5.2 Hub areas

These are the focal points or centre for group activities. Often they are not provided due to the lack of space, the use or perception of indoor/outdoor play, or extreme conditions and climatic concerns. In hotter climates they are a must because they can provide shade and, if well designed, airflow to help cooling. In cooler climates a large deciduous shade tree or a pergola where vines (e.g. Wisteria) are growing over the top will make a practical but visually attractive space. These should be meeting areas for parents and children on arrival, a space for group activity and a sense of being part of the community. A hub should be large enough to accommodate comfortably the number of people who will use it.

Having a visually attractive, comforting meeting space for children to arrive at in the morning is an important part of making them feel welcome. A hub space can provide a sense of acceptance and a point for getting to know other people, not only for the children, but for their families as well. It is a point to get together in the afternoons where the child and teacher can share the days' happenings.

The area needs to be welcoming not intimidating. It should be large enough for groups. A child seated on the ground should have a sense of enclosure and privacy but, when standing, be able to see the rest of the playground through the greenery.

The design should be one that can be utilised for a wide range of activities, such as the sharing of a birthday cake, morning tea, impromptu concerts or a place to sit and talk with friends.

This is a space that suggests a multitude of uses. If the space is too tight consideration can be given to extending verandahs – which, all too frequently, especially in hotter climates, are too narrow at 3m. Extending a verandah to a width of a minimum of 4 to 8m (if space will allow) will provide a valid connection between inside and outside areas. Long narrow spaces do not allow conducive grouping: the space needs to be like an outdoor playroom which also provides a valid connection between inside and outside play.

Figure 5.1 C&K Tarragindi War Memorial Kindergarten, Brisbane Australia: a shaded, sunken pit play area creates a defined play area but is also used heavily as a meeting point for children in the morning

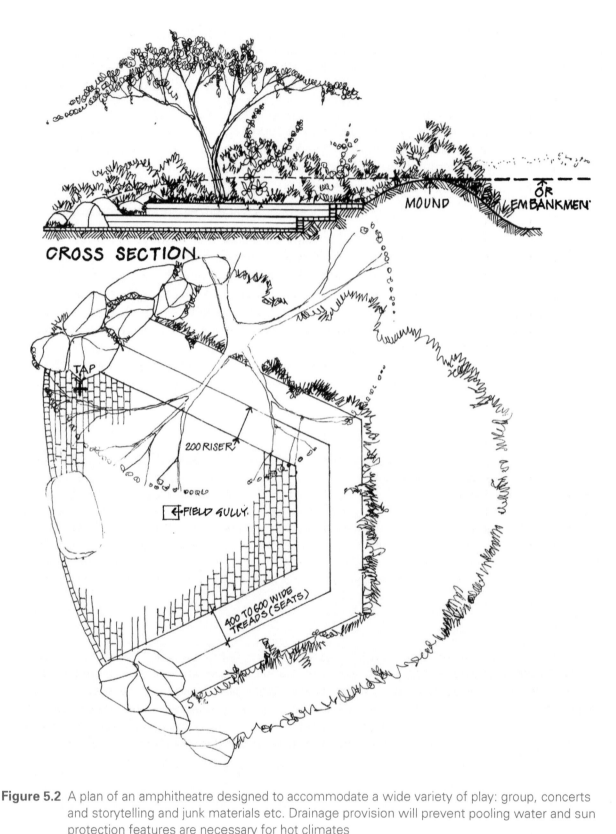

CROSS SECTION.

MOUND OR EMBANKMEN'

TAP

200 RISER

FIELD GULLY.

400 TO 600 WIDE TREADS (SEATS)

Figure 5.2 A plan of an amphitheatre designed to accommodate a wide variety of play: group, concerts and storytelling and junk materials etc. Drainage provision will prevent pooling water and sun protection features are necessary for hot climates

5.2.1 Design considerations

The suggestions below are all ideas that can be incorporated into the space. But note that careful assessment of the space and site is required to ensure the most practical and effective solution/s.

Consider the following:

▶ Siting: consider locating the hub adjacent to the building to support a flow of play between the inside and outside areas. In space-restricted playgrounds this can be part of a wide terrace or verandah. Locate the hub away from distracting noises such as traffic. Siting the hub adjacent to compatible play activities will support a natural progression and flow of play, for example a large freeform sand area with a continuous surface linking through to the hub space. Whether it is sited by the building, or in another part of the playground, it should be set aside from the main pedestrian traffic flow in order to minimise disturbance to children's play. In cold climates a sun catchment and wind protected area are essential. In hot climates provision for shade and exposure to cooling breezes is desirable, while most areas need summer shade and winter sun to provide year-round viability.

▶ Landform: for example, if an embankment area exists, consider building a mini-amphitheatre with views and shade trees over the top that will create an enriching outdoor hub space.

▶ Access: clearly define major access corridors. Provide a wide pathway leading directly to the edge of the hub area to ease access without causing unnecessary intrusion to activities taking place. Controlled access to a specific area (for example, a gazebo) will ensure ease of access without intrusion to the uninterrupted space within the gazebo. It will also be suitable for prams/buggies, trolleys and wheelchairs.

▶ Consider placing raised garden beds or railings with vertical slats (of approximately 650mm) around the edge of the hub space, particularly where there is a potential fall height beyond approximately 200mm.

▶ Size and scale: design the size of the hub according to the number of children who will be utilising the space at one time. Ideally, there should be enough space for the hub to be a rallying point for all. In a playground where large numbers of children are to be accommodated the inclusion of two adjoining areas in large playground should be considered. In moderate sized playgrounds the area should be approximately 20–30m² (particularly in a centre with a maximum of 75 children). Approximately 15m² of unencumbered space is just large enough for a group of 20 children. Use 1m² per child as a rough estimate for spaces that will need to cater for more than this. The final amount of space however, need to take into account the size of the playground and not compromise the delivery of the needed wide variety of play spaces.

▶ Shape: this will depend on space, but must provide for a group of children to play or sit for storytelling or to circulate around play activities such as a water trough. Rounded spaces are the most inviting. Squat square or rectangular spaces will suffice.

▶ Definition of the space: create a sense of semi-enclosure while at the same time ensuring that children have a partial view of the adjoining space. To achieve this use raised garden beds, embankments, boulders or retaining walls and planting, or perhaps a circular sunken play area with a stepped edge approximately 400mm deep that children can use as a seat.

▶ Planting: a wide variety of plants creates subtle sensory experiences in an area where children are less mobile and more likely to absorb these pleasures. Provide a large tree or clusters of trees to create a copse to help define the space. In colder climates deciduous trees allow for winter sun and provide a sensory stimulation through the changing seasons.

▶ Shade: this needs careful consideration based on the climate. Use deciduous trees in colder climates, deciduous vines or trees or pergolas in temperate climates, and evergreen trees with permanent fixed shade cover with evergreen vines, shade sails on rounded poles (not square, to avoid injury) or a more permanent open-sided fixed roof shelter with air vents/fans in tropical climates. All shade provision should take into account the impact of the shade provision on the adjoining areas. It can often be taken in the context of decisions about planting – so that a combination of shade and planting will help enhance different angles of sun shade that will occur during the year, particularly in hot climates. Other shelters can be used which are more like a thatched hut however, they could be destroyed in the event of a cyclone.

▶ Pergolas and gazebos: pergolas with pitched or flat roofs are a popular play space, particularly when on a slightly elevated deck, which further defines this as a separate area. Plant seasonal markers such as grape vines, wisteria or permanent dense shade for hotter climates.

▶ Surfaces: use hard surfaces due to the intended intense use. Exercise care in the placement of surface materials to ensure that they can be hosed and swept with ease. Do not have uneven surfaces that retain water or create a trip hazard. Careful choice and laying of surface materials will heighten the sensory richness of the space. To do this there needs to be subtle inclusion of changes in texture with only slight colour variations that do not distract from the green visual beauty of the space. Slight variations of texture and form will allow the children to walk with bare feet or sit on the surface with comfort. Consider using patterned brickwork, in swirls, squares or other shapes, paving, or compacted earth in small less densely used spaces. When concrete is used it needs to be broken up with, for example, edging strips, patterned paving, leaf imprints, Aboriginal symbols (for example kangaroo paw imprints) or glass mosaics. Cold climates with constantly damp surfaces may need to consider a large timber platform sited just above ground level for this area to ensure the extremes in climate will not inhibit extensive varied use.

▶ Supervision: ensure that teachers can look across the space to catch a glimpse of the children without necessarily intruding on their play. Use plants and other barriers to a height of approximately 500mm.

5.3 Quiet setting-up areas

In many respects quiet setting-up areas are smaller and often present as a smaller version of the hub area. Children will actively seek quiet, defined spaces of varying sizes from small, encapsulated spaces to larger, group areas. The design needs to ensure a visually attractive, enticing space that the children can own during their period of play.

The setting-up areas or small group getaways can be attached to a verandah or other covered outdoor space. Two or more of these areas can be incorporated in different parts of the playground to accommodate creative social play e.g. small gazebos, bamboo or curved willow hut. The aim is to create quiet retreat points where two or three children can play together in an uninterrupted group space away from the main melee and the larger number of children. It gives them time to quietly develop their own ideas without too much intrusion.

The use of loose parts in these areas will maximise the use of the space. Often, after observing the needs of a child or group of children, a teacher will produce several items out of the storage cupboard that suggest a different form of play, and can be sufficiently open-ended to act as a catalyst for children to pick up and utilise to fit in with their own play schemes.

5.3.1 Design considerations

Siting

Ideally, quiet areas should be sited adjacent to compatible play activities that support a natural progression and flow of play, for example a paved space extending from the sandpit area where a water trough may be set up, or a stepped terrace up to an area with a painting easel or where story times may happen.

Shape and size

Circular spaces work well. Choose a space at least 2–4m in diameter, or as large as 6m in diameter depending on the availability of space and the proximity of the adjoining facilities that can flow out into it. Define the space with large shade trees. A gazebo with hanging baskets can offer a sense of enclosure, or vines placed across the roof can give seasonal variation. Include shaded seating areas with curved seats that invite a level of social interaction and discussion.

Surfaces

Ideally use varied surfaces, such as circular paving, log rounds, brushed concrete with patterns set in around the periphery or in a central point. In a large playground where space is available

Figure 5.3 Enka School, Istanbul Turkey: gazebo space sited to the side of the main busy play area with a raised surface to elevate potentially cold surfaces. Used as an area for setting up play activities and for group play

compacted bare earth and a shaded tree getaway point can become a very enticing play space. Include clearly defined links to the adjoining spaces, preferably as a continuous surface, to make it easy to move toys or wheelchairs between them.

Planting and shade

Planting should be the most dominant feature of these spaces. Use a wide variety of trees. Install shade sails or fixed roof shelters particularly in hotter climates.

Adaptable use

The provision of loose parts allows for the extension and development of a wide variety of different forms of play and is designed to increase the potential of these areas enormously. Old curtains or hollow blocks become a castle, soft mats and cushions become a meeting area for reading books or puzzles, easels can be set up for painting or a box of chalk provided for pavement art or the building of structures out of smooth pebbles that children may have previously gathered.

5.4 Sandpits

Sandpits have a great capacity to arouse and sustain children's interest and enjoyment, are an essential component in an early childhood playground and offer the potential for a wide diversity of play. For younger children the initial play with sand is a simple exploration of material. This is a tactile experience that slowly develops from functional skills to far more complex and focused play which is further enhanced by the inclusion of self-selected loose parts.

Manipulative skills such as pouring, gentle digging and patting take place with sand and particularly with water. Loose parts tools provide opportunities for movement control and clear, separate roles for both hands aid the far reaching benefits needed for short- and long-term skills.

A large, welcoming, freeform sensory rich sandpit can be a focal point of the playground. At any one time this design can accommodate a variety of evolving forms of play and changing social configurations.

The location should take into account easy delivery of top-up sand and the position of a tap – for play and clean-up purposes.

Figure 5.4 C&K Tarragindi War Memorial Kindergarten, Brisbane Australia: wide, free flowing sandpit designed to accommodate different clusters of children who can play separately or merge at any one time. Wide sweeping edges allow for ease of access and a smooth surface for tipping and pouring and development of fine motor skills. There is easy access to stored play items for children to add to their play

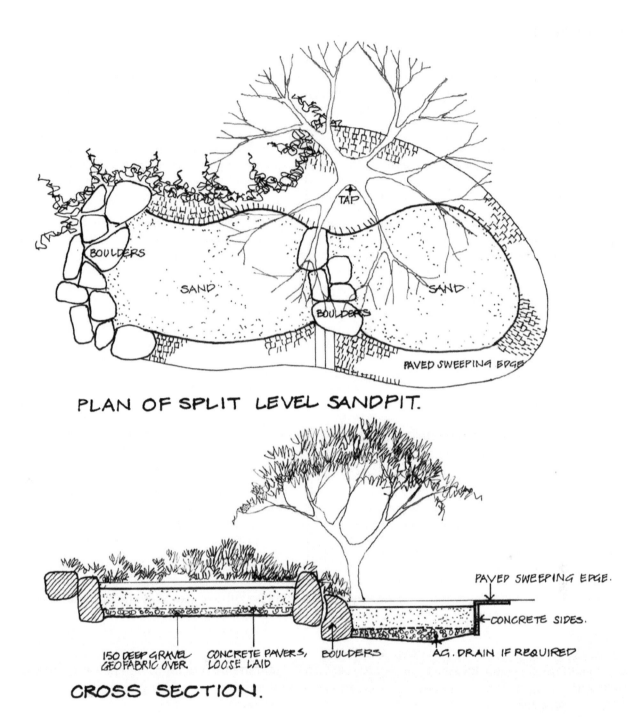

PLAN OF SPLIT LEVEL SANDPIT.

CROSS SECTION.

150 DEEP GRAVEL GEO FABRIC OVER.   CONCRETE PAVERS, LOOSE LAID   BOULDERS   AG. DRAIN IF REQUIRED

PAVED SWEEPING EDGE.
CONCRETE SIDES.

Figure 5.5 A sandpit built into a sloping embankment area allows for a large, free flowing sandpit with a flat play surface. Boulders are set into the adjoining embankment area which invites a variety of usage as varied as sitting, climbing and a surface for building items from sand

5.4.1 Design considerations

Sunken sandpits work very effectively in warm climates but will require drainage provision. In colder climates they may need to be raised on a timber platform to minimise the cold surfaces. Their design and location needs to ensure flow-out spaces from the sandpits whether it be a paved surface with bull-nosed edges or a large timber deck above ground level that finish flush with the top of the sandpit. Factors such as shade provision both fixed and seasonal and a location next to other facilities to support the flow of play all add impetus to play (see also Playgrounds for toddlers and babies, Chapter 9).

Consider the following:

► Siting: most sandpits are constructed to be below ground level. However, in some areas with poor drainage, rooftop playgrounds or in colder climates (where sandpits may freeze over in winter) it may be necessary to have above-ground containers (avoid high-sided containers as they are a trip hazard, lead to sand spillage and limit the play options).

► Shape: a freeform shape provides niche play spaces appropriate to the normal small group or solo play. Extra niches can be created by placing boulders or a low bench within the sandpit.

► Sandpit bed and drainage: a 1:100 slope is needed for drainage. A pit 750–800mm deep needs to be provided. Use a base of 150mm gravel or crushed rock, then a layer of geofabric with either pavers 50mm thick laid flat or heavy duty open weave plastic matting, then at least 600mm of sand. An agricultural pipes drainage system can be placed in the rubble in the base of the pit before linking to the stormwater system or drainage outlet will help enormously. In above-ground sandpits use geo-fabric below matting instead of rubble while ensuring a drainage outlet.

► Sand: choose sand that has a balanced mixture of particles ranging from very fine to coarse, but not more than 1.5mm for packing and moulding, for example white washed river sand or washed sand that is free of sediment so it will not stain. A simple method for checking this is to rub a piece of white cloth with wet sand. Avoid crushed stone as it is harmful to the eyes and can graze skin.

► Edges: use solid edges that prevent sand mixing with the soil in below-ground pits; preferably use bullnose bricks to minimise sharp edges, and as a flat surface for tipping and pouring. Ensure the edge is flush with the paved sandpit surrounds to assist sweeping the sand back into the pit, as well as facilitating the natural flow of play. In above-ground pits, use timber rounds for the edges and ensure these are flush with the surrounding timber deck.

► Shade: trees are an attractive natural solution, and deciduous varieties provide summer shade and welcome winter sun. They require maintenance: rake daily when leaves fall. Moveable shade covers work well. High-density shade cloth is ideal as it provides shade, is light and allows water to drip through, so the cover does not pool with water after rain. Alternatively, use fixed shelters that are no more than 2m high, placed to provide cover from mid-morning to mid-afternoon while allowing for early morning and late afternoon sunlight to dry the sand. Avoid using slatted timber roofs as they create a heavy shadow pattern that distracts play.

► Use rounded posts set into the round – not sharp angles as these can prevent head bumping hazards.

► Covers: there is no easy or foolproof way of covering sandpits to protect them from animal fouling or vandalism. Shade cloth covers held down by rubber tyres allow air to circulate freely and can be easily removed and replaced daily. This solution has proved to be one of the most practical ways to cover sand as it is easy to implement and cost effective. Wire on all sides of a sandpit is not recommended as it creates a cage-like effect.

5.5 Secret places

Secret places are the nooks and crannies, the hideaway spaces and the unexpected retreats that children seek out and discover independently. These are the spaces that meet a child's desire to get away, to be by themselves or to share time with a friend without interruption, where they can dream up ideas, play different roles and create objects with things as simple as pebbles and stones. They allow children to withdraw from the hustle and bustle, to sit and observe, to contemplate, to hide and dream, or even to calm down for a while before returning to the melee.

These spaces act as a catalyst for a child's imagination, resulting in colourful acting out of fantasy and dramatic play. Often these areas evolve in a natural setting created by the boughs of trees, the leaves on the ground and the bare earth, giving children the chance to observe nature at first hand. A child can sit and study ants and butterflies, touch leaves and bark and enjoy the smell of the damp earth.

Figure 5.6 Small cubby house built in a tree with a cloth added on a wet day. Seats can also be added
when requested to provide a quiet get-away space

When carefully handled these spaces can provide a wealth of multi-sensory stimulation that will
extend children's spatial awareness, interaction and their sense of self esteem by getting away
or sharing time with a friend. It is the tranquillity of the area that allows a child who has difficulty
with assimilation the opportunity of down-time or a place to reflect and observe.

Secret places can crop up anywhere within a playground where children find an under-utilised
nook or cranny. It can be the spontaneous use of a space under a bush, a small gap in a fence for
them to view out or a cool space under a deck on a hot day. With the support of loose parts and
a teacher's assistance when required, these can be some of the most heavily used creative
spaces in the playground.

5.5.1 Design considerations

Consider the following:

▶ Siting: often the development of secret places happens over time, through teachers observing a playground in terms of child preferences or identifying an underutilised space that – with some small pruning, some pebbles on the ground, additional planting or a mosaic painting (permanent or changeable) – may further enhance children's enjoyment of the space.

▶ Size: the key design characteristic of secret places is their variability. In size they can be 3–10m^2, or secret nooks of 0.5–1m^2. Some areas will be paved, others will use natural materials, and still others a perch on a boulder or log.

▶ Loose parts: in reality observation of children's use of the playground will soon reveal what they perceive as a loose part. The gathering of small round boulders to make their own small group space or the strategic placement of cardboard boxes are just two of the many approaches children will use. Where space will allow many of these areas can be established if children have access to loose parts.

▶ Vegetation: a favoured method for cooler climates is using planting to create secret spaces, whether it be a cluster of clumping bamboo where a small hidey hole has been cut in between or the spaces underneath a drooping willow.

Figure 5.7 Hidden nooks to discover can be created out of mounded earth, long, spindly clusters of trees and low ground covers. Water troughs can be added as requested

Open play areas

6.1 Why children need open play areas

The nature of physical play is directly related to the child's level of motor-control. The provision of space helps the major development of walking, running, climbing and jumping. In the open area children can experience the sheer joy of undertaking a wide diversity of gross-motor activities such as running, tumbling, rolling, hopping, skipping and jumping, and build up their fine-motor skills. Open play areas, combined with loose parts and adaptable equipment, will enable children's play to progress markedly in a variety of different solo or group sizes.

This is also a place for pretend and open-ended play where children can wish and make temporary changes to a setting using loose parts and in the process sustain their interest and enjoyment of the open space. Changing levels such as accessible embankments and mounds extend the physical play in this area.

For children resting between bouts of energetic play, provide shelter and informal seating at the periphery. This could be in the form of deciduous or evergreen trees, or even an extended shelter structure. Consider whether a drinkable water source is needed (see Chapter 8 loose parts).

6.2 Elements of an open play area

The main areas to consider are:

► Open areas: an open flat running space in the form of a large rectangle, square or circle centrally located in the playground can be a focal point that links to all other parts of the play space. In tight playgrounds, low, narrow grassed areas that extend from one end of the play space to the other are often used as a connection point between different section of the playground. It is the short narrow spaces where speed cannot be built up that place the most constraint on children's freedom of choice.
► Mounds: the provision of mounds offers challenging surfaces to run up and down and views to beyond.
► Terracing: changes in level can provide an extension to play. In a gently inclined space the building of low level terraces (no more than 500mm) connecting different areas creates a subtle sub-division of space and an area to jump and balance on, or a lookout point from a quiet play area down into the open running space. A site with steep inclines and large open spaces is an ideal setting for this type of play area as it provides a playground where enormous challenge is provided without the risk of vertical falls.
► Changes in level: changes of 3 to 5m can be divided into split level playground spaces that will work effectively for older children if the spatial provision will allow. Ensure that the design eliminates any risk of vertical falls of more than 500mm.
► Embankments: these offer a sound solution where steep level changes exist in a larger playground or to the side of smaller playground. Ensure a range of ways for children to get up and down them, such as rubber tyre steps, scramble walls, rounded smooth boulders or slides. Be creative about where embankments can be installed. In practice, the cost of a 3m high retaining wall with structural integrity and associated drainage to create a boring playground wall can cost more than a stepped embankment with play, safety and enjoyment features. There is a marked safety benefit in developing an effective angled embankment wall approximately 2.5 to a maximum 3m in height with an angled incline of no steeper than 30° or less, with multiple different forms of access and egress that provide challenge whilst lowering the major risk of a vertical fall.

6.3 Open spaces

The open play area if well sited and proportioned provides a vitally important hub and linkage flow of space to all parts of the playground. It can support more than just running distances or playing at chasing. With the use of movable equipment and loose parts, a wide variety of agility-with-speed play can occur. This space is the heart of the open play activities which relates to moving at speed.

Clearly the open space will always assist supervision, both viewing and pedestrian. The teacher can observe children's play and quickly move to support, guide or intervene if necessary.

6.3.1 Design considerations

Consider the following:

► Site: flat open areas when located in a central position act as a focal hub which will allow children and teachers to observe and cut across to quieter spaces within the playground. The hub will be the central point of activity preferably designed with access leading to the periphery of the space and the wider playground area. The viability of this however, can often be curtailed by the shape and form of the play space and may require the creative use of different levels or areas within the playground.

► Size and shape: whilst ideally there should be a large area with a flat surface to allow for easy, speedy running and movable equipment to be set up, a ¼ to 1/3 of the total playground should be used for this purpose depending on site characteristics. Preferably it will have a squat shape and should be at least a minimum of 15m in length to provide enough space for children to build up speed and momentum. If the playground size and form does not allow for this, there are often many options planning and design can provide whilst keeping in mind children's needs. Long narrow spaces will allow children to build up speed and act as a tract throughout the play area and an angled section of earth will provide an area where they can run up and down.

► Surface: well-maintained lawns in a sunny position are actively sought and are a clear preference of many children as they run, fall, tumble, roll and enjoy the feel and smell of the grass. Bare earth mixed with sand under shaded trees can also work effectively in other areas. All natural surfaces need retaining and maintenance. Budgets should set aside funding for patching, aerating, fertilising and top-dressing lawn spaces. Many of these tasks can be done by some of the children. Check that there is no pooling of water after rain. In tight playgrounds artificial grass is often the only solution to maintaining a surface particularly where there is high density usage and nothing else will survive.

Figure 6.1 An open running space with low mounds will extend gross motor skills. Mounds create a lookout point during imaginative play, a linking point for planks and jouncing boards and extra challenge to play where children run up and over the mounds

6.4 Mounds

The inclusion of mounds to offer a change in level, the gentle inclines of landform and the steep embankments of major changes in level all create natural elements that with careful enhancement can provide even in some of the tightest playgrounds a marked extension and enjoyment to play.

Long low mounds or groups of mounds of varying heights are often a useful and heavily used agility structure. When assessing the need to build mounds take into account the size and existing features of the playground site. Only when natural slopes and embankments are not available should these areas be considered in smaller more compact playgrounds as they can take up a lot of room which may restrict the variety needed to accommodate varied play needs.

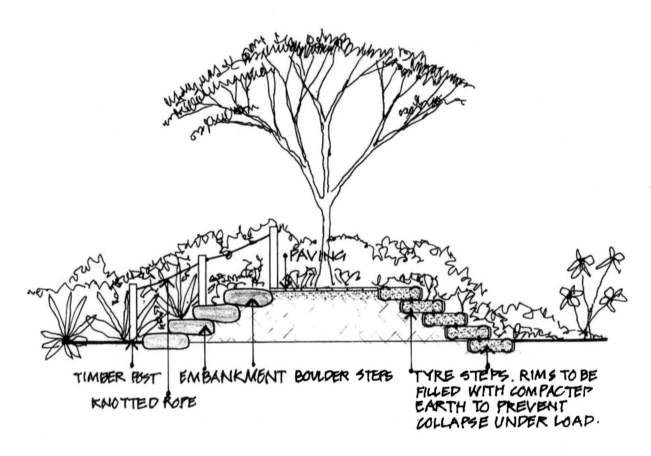

Figure 6.2 Stepped garden mounds break up a flat and otherwise boring play area by creating a lookout point, a climbing surface and a place to enjoy the sensory richness of the surrounding planting

6.4.1 Design considerations

Consider the following:

▶ Size: the height of mounds should vary according to the amount of space available and the age and size of the child users. Very high mounds will dominate and will often create an imbalance in the playground. If available, however, if up to approximately 1.5m they will be well utilised particularly by older children and will allow staff to have partial supervision of children on the other side of the mound. If space is restricted a smaller mound of the playground has been designed specifically for younger children, a smaller combination of mounds approximately 1.3m will still provide a surface for children to run up and over as well as a structure on which to place planks and build-up an obstacle course. If in clusters children can run up and over them at different angles and speeds.

▶ Slope: mounds are workable with a 30° of slope. They require careful construction and constant maintenance to help minimize problems caused by constant wear and tear. A well compacted solid soil base that does not have easily exposed gravel or other abrasive material, covered with a layer of top soil approximately 120–150mm deep, is required. This mound should not be used until the grass is well established and has been top dressed and firmly compacted.

▶ Surface: heavy-duty grass, or rubber matting through which grass can grow, are recommended, as they help retain the soil and prevent erosion, whilst providing a slightly softer surface for children to play on. Gradual slopes which retain soil and are easier to mow facilitate maintenance.

Variations to a basic mound include:

▶ Clusters of mounds: can be of different heights to create challenge and interest. A cluster needs to have a slightly raised area in the middle to prevent water pooling.
▶ Steps: made of in-ground rubber tyres or horizontal logs can add a play or access point.
▶ Viewing point(s): these can be enhanced by paving on top of the mound (1/2 to 1m^2).

6.5 Embankments

Not all playgrounds will be able to have play embankments, but conversely some steep sites are perfect. Earthworks may be necessary to create a uniform slope (so as to eliminate vertical falls). The challenge comes from the design of access and egress play options, which can be varied to suit different levels of competencies.

Figure 6.3 Enka School, Istanbul Turkey: height and challenge without the risk of vertical falls creates an embankment with multiple ways to climb up and down. Heavily used by children seeking a variety of different ways to access and egress the embankment

6.5.1 Design considerations

Consider the following:

▶ Size: embankments can be up to 3 or 4m high or more if terracing is incorporated to allow for challenge as well as a resting point. The higher they are, the more the children enjoy them; embankments of only 1.5–2m will still be enjoyed but may not sustain the interest of 4- to 5-year-old children over time.

▶ Vegetation: this is important for shade, screening, aesthetics and depending on the type of planting used can further help to stabilise the embankment. Consider narrow stepped gardens for low level planting with boulder rises or shaded trees with spreading canopies (ensure the children cannot climb or swing on them due to their location). Very steep sections of an embankment may need to be heavily planted and fenced off; risk management education of the children will be needed.

▶ Surface: to prevent erosion, the entire face of a play embankment should be surfaced – but with active play options, not structures just for retaining purposes. The play options are permanently fixed (not movable) and could include:

  ▷ stairs with a handrail;
  ▷ rubber tyre steps;
  ▷ a large long slippery slide with a flat top, high sides and a run off area at the base set into the earth;
  ▷ log scramble walls with knotted ropes;
  ▷ poles set into an embankment at ground level with a rope above so that children can climb and hold on to ropes at a high level. Two placed together will often result in the task being shared with a friend, or walk up it with legs splayed and holding on to a rope at the top;
  ▷ steep boulder stairs weaving in and out of the existing vegetation with a rope handrail to assist the less agile and younger children. In practice I have found that the ropes eventually protect the garden as children scramble up the embankments making their own courses through the area;
  ▷ paved flat lookout areas at the top with seats if space will allow so that children can sit back, observe and socialise with one another;
  ▷ scramble nets (openings of less than 90mm).

Figure 6.4 Tugulawa Early Education, Brisbane Australia: redevelopment of a playground on a tight steep and narrow sites. Embankment offers children a variety of usage through the inclusion of rubber tyre steps and a scramble wall and a ramp leading to a cubby house with views across the playground. Also features a sunken cubby house underneath

All of these fittings need to be set down into the surface of the embankment – bolted in with concrete footings with engineering advice used to ensure that they are structurally sound. It is essential that protruding bolts are not present as they can cause injury. The surface materials preferably need to finish flush with the embankment surface to make a compatible accessible system even for very young children.

The finishing point for the lower level should be flush with the ground surface or raised no more than 150–200mm, so that as children slow their momentum they can readily put their feet on the ground.

In a steep high part of the embankment, careful design and checking by an engineer can produce some much favoured results. For example slides on two levels with an intermediary deck large enough to cope with three or four children and a starting point for the slide from the upper level the deck to one side, and start again on the opposite side of the deck so they can slow down momentum, get on their feet and transfer across to the other side. Railings of at least 750mm and if wished vertical slat in-fills no more than 90mm apart can be an added safety precaution for the platform. Ladders could be substituted for the 2-stage slides.

If in doubt about installing some of the activity elements, consult an engineer. Ensure regular checking of items which may deteriorate over time, like rope handrails, scramble nets, log inserts.

It is essential to remember that trees should be included as they provide essential summer shade and a visual break-up of space and provide an attractive area. The inclusion of deciduous trees in cooler climates can stimulate children's interest in seasonal change with the falling leaves. Embankments should never be seen as just an area for fast play.

6.6 Access and pathways

Pathways can open up spaces to create access and egress throughout the playground and in the process provide a vastly varied range of opportunities. As Jim Greenman (2005 and 1988) puts it: 'Pathways are the routes commonly taken, not necessarily planned. Outside walkways are the official paths; dirt paths worn into the grass are unofficial but no less real.'

Figure 6.5 Tugulawa Early Education, Brisbane Australia: the upper level of the extended playground provides a pathway and viewing area to the sandpit in the lower section of the playground; access to a watercourse and digging patch in the foreground and swings in the far left corner

At their most practical level pathways assist parents and children entering the centre, help staff with viewing, observing and assisting children. Open play areas need path systems. These provide both play opportunities and access to all other parts of the playground, and from the building to the playground. Paths should allow children to choose visually, and then move easily to a play point without distracting other children at play.

Correctly placed, pathway systems provide end-to-end access within the playground – an essential service for movement of children and loose parts in a manner which does not interrupt existing play. Path systems also support rapid pedestrian access for teachers in their supervisory role.

Figure 6.6 Tugulawa Early Education, Brisbane Australia: embankment play area that incorporates rubber tyre steps, scramble wall, slippery slide, hand-ropes for less agile children and boulder steps

There also needs to be a path system around the periphery of the central open space area – for both direct play and to link up with existing paths in other areas of the playground. Although normally flush with the ground surface, some portions may need to be elevated; for example when linking two levels, a ramp may be needed or even a bridge over a drain or watercourse. Variations will be site dependant.

MARBLES RANDOMLY
PLACED WITHIN CONCRETE
SLAB SO THAT ONLY 1/4
OF THE BALL IS VISIBLE.

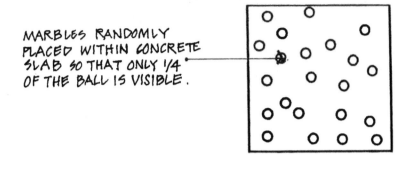

DRAW OR IMPRINT SHAPES
AND TEXTURES OF LEAVES,
BARK, TWIGS AND OTHER
EXAMPLES AS REQUIRED

IMPRINT WITH LARGE AND
SMALL CORRUGATED SHEET
METAL PATTERNS. VARY
THE SPACING AND WIDTH
OF THE TWO CORRUGATED
PATTERNS.

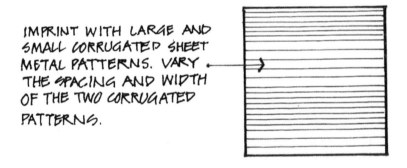

Figure 6.7 Examples of materials used for a main pathway system. They can be utilised at the entry to a centre or the main playground pathway links and are particularly suited to heavy traffic pathways

6.6.1 Design considerations

Things to keep in mind with the planning are:

▶ major access corridors between the inside and outside areas;
▶ links to the periphery of open, quiet and active areas;
▶ gentle placing of compatible play activities next to each other with perhaps a small pathway link e.g. a pathway to a chook house with a link to a gazebo and then the sandpit, an inclined pathway through a cluster of trees, provision of steps to enable steeper level of change to occur, the linking through to an item such as a slippery slide flowing down an embankment and then linking back to another part of the pathway system. The final outcome is one of variety, different forms and space suggesting varied usage without dominating the space. Above all the pathways system must be a subtle gentle inclusion within a predominantly natural environment;

- surfaces for this area ideally should always vary, depending on the amount of space available. Main corridor pathway systems which are wide and visually attractive enough will create a welcoming access between inside and outside spaces;
- in tropical climates provision of a pathway in the form a shallow swale drain will allow for rapid clearance of surface water during heavy rain;
- surface changes that indicate different usage of a potential area e.g. a patterned paved pathway leading to a circular paved shaded area, sensory pathways with leaf imprints, inset pebble or marbles to catch the light;
- inclusion of stairs possibly with varied markings along the front of the steps particularly if visually impaired children are to use the space;
- alternatively, surface levels that vary in form and height so that wheeled toys can be pushed throughout the area and surface change enjoyed and experienced;
- slowing of momentum though the inclusion of galvanised iron imprinted into wet concrete surfaces;

6.7 Wheeled toy pathways

Paths and path systems can also facilitate the use of wheeled toys such as:

- wheeled toys with three wheels;
- wheeled toys with two wheels;
- tricycles with an added hook for trolleys or a dinky seat or stand on the back;
- scooters to cope with the changes in skill levels – start with a four wheel, then progress to a three wheeled scooter and then a two wheel scooter;
- prams;
- wheelbarrows with two wheels;
- four wheeled trolleys.

In particular, bicycles and tricycles are a preferred play option of children. Despite the excellent advantages of the sheer fun and physical development that bicycles provide, a dominance of bicycles is not recommended as they inhibit a broader form of play and the ensuing developmental opportunities provided. A dominance of bicycles in a playground at all times of the day must be seen as an example of limited play planning and outdoor programming – sadly this shows a limited perception of children's needs.

Figure of eight pathways restrict the form and level of play and soon result in boredom where too often where the only thrill becomes the crashing at the junction point! Free-flowing main pathways with varied surfaces linked to smaller areas (when the space will allow) create special ambiences with flow-off paths to specific spaces create ambience and mystery of hidden spaces that invite varied usage particularly when variations in the textures and forms are the tools for inviting use of these spaces. This does not mean that this potentially excellent provision should not be included, but the available space, design of the playground and the level of allowed usage must be taken into consideration.

6.7.1 Design considerations

Consider the following:

- Location: the main track often works effectively when it is located around the periphery of the central area. But at the ends, or on offshoots, there can be small retreats and turning points e.g. a narrow section of pathway that goes off and around to a cluster of trees or around a boulder garden bed at the base of a tree. Consider also turning circles where there is sufficient space for children to turn the bicycles around and go back to another area, or where temporary signs can be put up if usage will be too markedly intrusive to other play activities in that area occurring at that time (e.g. portable stop signs, slow down etc). Do not put these in permanently as it presents a closed play option; but use these as an opportunity to teach road rules.

▶ Surface: install varied surfaces. Usually the main track will be concrete and smooth, because it will be used by children withwheeled carts and trolleys, and also act as an access point for all users and vehicles. But even here variations can be constructed; for example, a row of pavers along the edge can prompt different forms of balance. Other variations could be gentle speed bumps using imprinted corrugated iron, a slightly raised timber edge painted white to help children learn to steer, a sensory pathway (with imprinted textured leaves, imprint of animal or bird footprints, shells, children's footprints, culturally significant items) to add interest for the less speedy riders on offshoot tracks, and different paver patterns, rammed earth or even different colours to signal the entry to specialised activity areas.

CHAPTER 7

Active play areas

7.1 The need for active play

Exercise comes naturally to children aged 2–5 years: they enjoy the independence of moving about and selecting an increasingly wider range of activities. At times their energy seems unlimited. From the progression of crawling babies to holding onto railings and side stepping along, toddlers acquire an increasing level of sophistication of skills from their second year through to five years and beyond. This is a stage of perfecting gross muscular skills of running, walking, jumping, pushing, pulling and rolling. The desire for more complex skills soon increases, involving throwing, hanging, balancing, skipping, hopping, vertical climbing, descending, spinning and balancing, all of which are needed for building up physical control of legs, back and upper torso.

Figure 7.1 Tugulawa Early Education, Brisbane Australia: maximising spatial provision within a tight area with a high cubby with ramp access and a sunken hidey hole underneath

It is a time of exciting transition from the mastery of large muscles to the fine-tuning of small muscle groups of feet and hands. This extends to attaining the ability for swift changes of movement and direction following a sequence of activities, and mastery of fluidity and movement.

The acquisition of these skills influences other areas of development and has a powerful impact on how children interact with their environment. Cognitive skills will emerge as a child thinks through the next course of busy action: why the swing spins, how they can best hang upside down and how fast they can run. This development is observed by Anita M Trancik and Gary W Evans (1995):

> Well designed physical environments encourage the development of increased personal competency, allow children to perform at their current level of abilities, while at the same time pushing them to practice more skills.

Much of the play that happens in the active area will manifest itself in bursts of intense activity, punctuated by sudden slow-downs as children catch their breath, change direction or simply watch other active children, before bursting once more into busy activity. Other play will be of a highly imaginative type, with children acting out ideas and fears, or pretending and playing out different roles during dramatic play. Some of these play spells may be brief, while in other activities, such as dramatic play, there are often long periods of deep concentration and sustained activity, particularly as children get older.

Social configuration for this type of play will also vary, from the child who single-mindedly perfects a physical skill by repeated action, to pairs and groups of children who, by the age of five years, will be interacting with an increasingly high level of cooperation during play. The active area also provides an outlet for controlled aggression, a chance to use rough and tumble skills in an appropriate setting; a chance to use busy physical skills in a wide variety of uses including tumbling and rolling around together. These activities also allow children to learn when to stop to consider the feelings of the other parties and whether they are being too rough and in the process learn to take turns, share and not putting others at risk during busy play.

New levels of cognitive development will emerge, as will representative thinking (the capacity to think about things and their properties without taking immediate action) and complexive thinking, which is a chain of ideas not always in logical sequence. This has a large bearing on how a young child's play will develop: practise of these skills in the playground is vital if a child is to master them and maintain their interest and motivation.

The nature of the play in the active area can make it potentially the highest-risk area of the playground. Concerns about safety need to be balanced, ensuring a challenging stimulating space that will acknowledge and promote children's mastery of skills but ensure a setting which allows for modification and subtle changes to the setting to ensure that mastery is not followed by boredom and allows for supportive teaching to further enhance its use.

7.2 Selecting fixed equipment

Play in active areas can be facilitated through the careful selection of a limited number of fixed pieces of equipment, which can help to maximise the play options available to children.

Too often early childhood playgrounds are dominated by well-intentioned but ill-informed purchases that fail to meet the ongoing play needs of children in a supervised setting. These pieces of equipment languish in playgrounds as monuments to misunderstanding, for the following reasons:

▶ The equipment is often purchased regardless of how large it is and what space is available. This usually means that more varied play facilities cannot be provided.
▶ The siting is not carefully considered. In a tight space, supervision and access can be inhibited, as can the essential provision of being able to add movable equipment, so the structure's full potential cannot be realised. Children can be put at unnecessary risk when a standard

structure does not allow sufficient space around. By placing it too close to other fixed equipment items it leaves insufficient space for movable equipment or insufficient clearance of equipment with movable parts, for example flying foxes and swings. Site specific and carefully considered tailor-made simple adaptable structures are often the only solution (see Chapter 8 loose parts).

▶ The play value and its suitability for use in an early childhood centre playground, as distinct from a park, has not been fully assessed. Often the new equipment provides the same play options as equipment already in the public playground and presents a closed play option, meaning that it cannot have movable elements linked on and off it.

Figure 7.2 Enka School, Istanbul Turkey: resting decks between a series of interconnected activity bars some with fixed items e.g. monkey bar or others with hooks and the potential for changing the range of fittings e.g. looped nets and suspended bars for hanging off

To help decide what fixed equipment might be appropriate for a particular setting, think about the following:

▶ Does the equipment help develop better coordination so that children can acquire gross muscular skills of climbing, swinging, hanging, spinning, jumping, balancing and crawling?
▶ Does the equipment give the children a sense of real movement in their bodies so that they can feel the exhilaration of sliding down a slide or whizzing along on a flying fox or going up into the air on a swing?
▶ Does it heighten their sense of spatial awareness so that they can distinguish options of in and out, up and down, under and over, left and right, or appreciate the three-dimensional effect of a semi-enclosed space?

- ▶ Will this promote vestibular and proprioceptor function of play which provides the children with information regarding the direction and speed of movement and in the process help them to develop muscle tone and balance to help them progress from clumsy to coordinated as they take on the challenge of moving in space?
- ▶ Can children use the equipment as an adjunct to their dramatic play?
- ▶ Is its form flexible enough to inspire ongoing vibrant concentrated play and accommodate a variety of roles children may want to act out?
- ▶ Will the equipment let children use it not only alone but with others so that they can share a slide, compete to see who climbs up and down the quickest, or play together at height with relative safety or enjoy the sharing of swinging together?

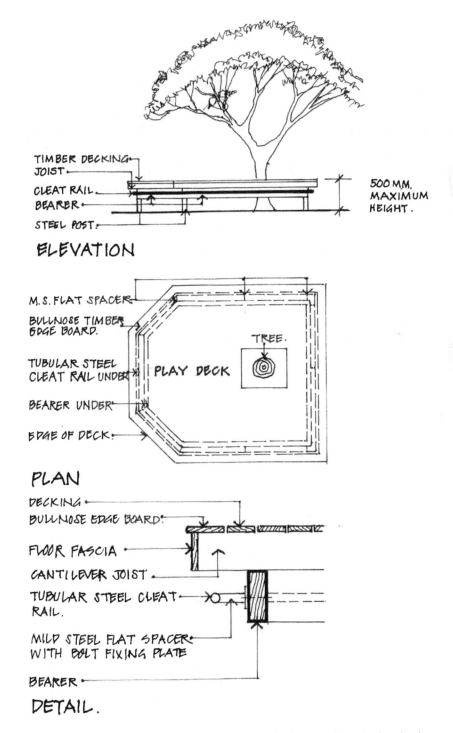

Figure 7.3 Cleat rails recessed under the deck allow planks with cleat ends to be hooked on and off to build obstacle courses with loose parts, e.g. ropes, planks, ladders, rubber tyres etc. Note: the cleat rail must be recessed under the deck so that it does not create a leg entrapment point.

7.3 Examples of popular fixed equipment

This section covers fixed structures that have a proven record of high levels of use. They are capable of sustaining children's interest and extending a wide range of skills to accommodate a diversity of play. It is the development of these basic structures and the combined use of additional movable equipment (such as trestles and loose parts) that will provide an open-ended setting that can be adapted and extended by children with staff to sustain their ongoing interest.

If the structures only offer static options then the children will inevitably think up unconventional and usually unsafe ways to use them, for example, climbing a fence or throwing an item at another child (negative patterns of a bored but spirited child). The activity structures in an early childhood facility need to meet children's needs, and this means that the equipment required is likely to differ from the off-the-shelf structures so common in public parks.

7.3.1 Platforms

Play platforms can be the most adaptable and accessible of items, which can encourage a wide variety of group play and sustain use for long periods. The two main forms of play platform structures that work effectively are low-level platforms and a series of interconnected stepped platforms of varying heights.

Low-level platforms can provide adaptable spaces with the potential for a wide variety of uses. They can be:

▶ a square or squat rectangular configuration that will allow small groups of children to congregate;
▶ a bench that is placed around the base of a tree to cover and protect the tree roots while giving the children a play surface: note that if the platform around the tree is narrow it will result in children running round repetitively as distinct from using it for a greater variety of play.

They can be located in a wide variety of settings which by location alone will suggest different levels and forms of play. For example, they can be placed in a large soft fall surface area and be the starting point for a wide diversity of uses for portable obstacle courses of varying sizes and forms using both junk materials and movable equipment. They can also be the link in the playground by being sited:

▶ immediately adjoining a rope bridge frame with adjustable rope fittings with potential for linking a variety of different items that can connect directly onto the platform or cleated timber;
▶ at the furthest point immediately adjoining a compatible play area which acts as a transition for play, for example adjoining a sandpit;
▶ alongside a low terraced area to provide an alternative access between levels;
▶ away from the main play space to enable quieter, varied forms of play.

Stepped platforms are a series of interconnected platforms that provide challenge and diversity as well as an observation point for those who wish to see the view from a height and work out how they will move between the varying levels. This is vital for the thrill of challenge that will lead to ongoing development of skills and risk assessment.

When deciding on stepped platforms, consider the following:

▶ Locate them away from main traffic flow routes and ensure that there is ample space around the platforms for moveable equipment to be added with ease.
▶ Incorporate large platforms with small, narrower platforms at a lower level that can be used as connection points for portable items, for example rope bridge frames, side stepping ropes or monkey bars.
▶ Create a series of small, interconnected platforms up to an embankment area, rather than a dominant, fixed structure.
▶ Ensure these high-risk areas are easy to supervise with clear viewing of, and access to, all fixed and movable climbing structures.

▶ Ensure there is a free-fall distance around the platform of at least 2m.

▶ Include several exit and entry points from a platform or other structure to prevent blockage at a height when several children are using the structure. These will allow more play options to suit varied skill levels, and to enable nervous children to change access points or reverse direction.

▶ Entry and exit points can be in the form of ladders with hand-grips, log scramble walls with a knotted rope, fireman's pole, cleat rails on the lower structures. Include eye-bolts on the underside of the deck where they can be readily clicked on and off using carabiner hooks.

▶ Site platforms close to where movable equipment items are stored to allow for easy access and additions to play.

Children will actively seek to extend these platforms and this can be done using loose parts. This may initially need to be done with the support of teachers to develop a perception of safety.

Dimensions should be checked to ensure compliance with local playground standards safety requirements.

Figure 7.4 A simple four post structure that can be placed in varying numbers either separately or interconnected. A variety of attachments will extend play. Note: concept drawing only for a simple four post structure.

7.3.2 Swings

Swings need a lot of space, but they support a surprising array of skill developments, some of which are quite complex. As well as any relevant playground standards, consider the following points when determining how to incorporate swings into a children's centre play space:

▶ Install a swing where multiple different seats can be attached or removed altogether. In most facilities, this can be achieved through the inclusion of high quality secured metal hooks attachment points that allow for a wide range of swing assemblies to be hooked on and off.

▶ In cold climates choose a sunny position, and ensure shade cover for hotter climates.

▶ Choose a flat site located away from the main routes or from other structures for safety reasons.

▶ Create barriers (with an access point), such as a raised garden bed, low shrubs, smooth tree trunks or even boulders (no more than 600mm high so that it remains easy for teachers to supervise) to prevent a child running into the swing area.

▶ Avoid swing seats with hard, narrow edges as these are more likely to cause an injury.

▶ If attaching the swing to a tree, make sure the branch is firm and strong enough to carry the weight of several children, and that the height of the branch does not result in a very wide swing arc, which younger children can be reluctant to use.

▶ Check with an arborist to establish whether a tree will support an eye-bolt screwed into a tree trunk. This can be the linking point for a suspended assembly e.g. a tyre and rope. By using eye-bolts in carefully selected tree trunks there is every likelihood that you will minimise the risk of stripping the bark and damaging the tree.

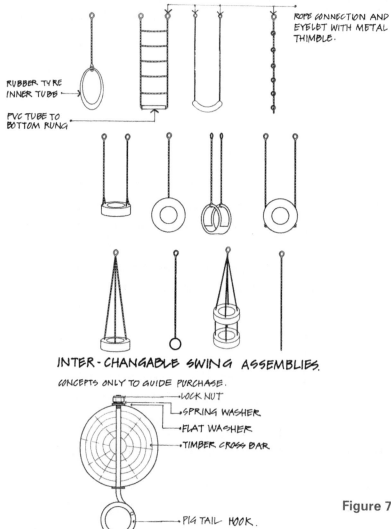

RUBBER TYRE INNER TUBE

PVC TUBE TO BOTTOM RUNG

ROPE CONNECTION AND EYELET WITH METAL THIMBLE.

INTER-CHANGABLE SWING ASSEMBLIES.

CONCEPTS ONLY TO GUIDE PURCHASE.

LOCK NUT
SPRING WASHER
FLAT WASHER
TIMBER CROSS BAR

PIG TAIL HOOK.

PIGTAIL HOOK DETAIL.

Figure 7.5 A pigtail hook set into the timber crossbars of a swing will allow a wide range of swing assemblies to be used

Figure 7.6 Enka School, Istanbul Turkey: timber swing frame with pigtail hooks

7.3.3 Flying foxes

A well-designed flying fox can be a source of challenge and enjoyment allowing a young child to sense their body flying through the air while acquiring new skills and a feeling of mastery over their actions.

The final choice of whether or not to include a flying fox will depend on the space available as locating one in a tight playground can overwhelm the variety and diversity of play elements needed within the total play space.

When assessing the suitability of a flying fox consider the following (in addition to any relevant standards) so that the end result meets the children's needs:

▶ Assess whether the play space is big enough: a flying fox is not recommended for a small playground because it takes up a large area and needs to be placed away from any traffic flow, often parallel to a fence.
▶ Use the flying fox to link different parts of the play space.
▶ Keep in mind the age of the children who will be using it and scale the design accordingly.
▶ Use mounds for the starting and finishing points as they will allow children of differing heights to move away from the start and finish with their feet firmly on the ground.
▶ Make the starting point approximately 800mm to 1 metre higher than the finishing point.

For further reference regarding flying fox usage refer to Chapter 10, Playgrounds for children with special needs, Section 10.4.6 on page 112.

CHAPTER 8

Loose parts

8.1 Why loose parts are important for play

For many adults loose parts are the leftovers, the wasted materials, messy leaves, the worn-out items that have no further use. However, for children it is often the case that 'one person's junk is another's treasure'. Simon Nicholson (1971) writes that:

> In any environment, both the degree of inventiveness and creativity, the possibility of discovery, are directly proportional to the number and kinds of variables in it.

In this chapter, loose parts refers to movable equipment (commercial and non-commercial) and junk and recycled materials.

When a new item is introduced to the children, it suggests a fresh activity and sparks a wave of enthusiasm for how it can be built into their creative play. For this process to work well, the changes need to create a pattern of ongoing challenge. The level of change can vary from subtle to large, depending on the children's needs.

Some items, such as a garden hose or a large flowerpot have a predictable use for gardening. Others such as a spoon, a bell or a trolley or a smooth small rock, will have a portable use. At other times the items may not – to the outsider – suggest any particular form of use. Instead, they are a catalyst for children's ideas which will evolve and expand as they explore and imagine how items can be used or fit in with what they are doing. For many, this may include the process of demolition: in the practice of creativity and discovery, it is not the finished product that dominates children's play.

Figure 8.1 Portable art easels can be used in a variety of settings. Can be used either as a blackboard with chalk or with paper secured with clips

It is this diversity of material that truly addresses children's needs. And it is the chemistry between physical settings and loose parts that enhances children's play and the teaching within it. The setting up of a playground has much to do with creating successful use of loose parts. The combination of small and large adaptable spaces combined with loose parts ensures that the use can be subtly changed to continue to meet children's needs.

One of the real benefits of movable equipment and items is that the user can take advantage of opportunities. This can be as simple as setting up an activity in a sunny, sheltered position on a cool day, or more complicated such as linking items to fixed structures to create an obstacle course or a water slide down a mound out of an old conveyor belt. Flexibility of use is the key to play and development-based learning.

The most obvious examples of areas with a heavy use of small loose parts are sandpits, digging patches and water. These are the areas where you will find a flower on a toy bulldozer, mud castles on the edge of a watercourse, and tunnels under a sandcastle. When this approach is taken throughout the playground, children receive a rich and rewarding outcome through an environment filled with exciting and sustained play opportunities. This form of play is the catalyst for increasing complexity of the activities being undertaken.

8.2 Selecting loose parts

The selection of loose parts is in itself a response to children's wishes and needs. This has to be combined with an appreciation of and visual eye for the natural environment and the items that will attract children's interest.

It should be noted that:

▶ Presenting too many items at once can be overpowering and not result in focused play, while too few items leaves children understimulated.
▶ Some items will be used daily; others will be kept in storage so that they can be brought out and used to assist a child's play project or act as a catalyst to a child's inquiry.
▶ What may seem to be junk to an adult may well prove to be a treasure and a catalyst to play for children, and may be more valuable than catalogue items – choose them based on children's needs.
▶ Some items (such as a jouncing board or a swing assembly) can be expensive, while others (such as junk or recycled items) can be cheap; still others are free (flowers, dappled sunshine) – incorporating cheap loose parts is a far more effective use of a budget than the bulk purchase of expensive items.

The selection and use of the smaller, loose parts should always take into account the potential of multiple uses. For example, a wheeled trolley is useful to carry blocks, tools, or even children, whereas a wheeled tricycle is less versatile. Instead of six bicycles of the same design, subtle variations of different types of wheels, a stand-on bar or a hook for carting items will ensure varied use. It is rare for older children to all want to play with the same thing – this is a pattern of younger childhood, which means when they are older they do not want or need 15 shovels or 20 ropes.

Some of the multiple uses can be:

▶ An old saucepan may be used to make pretend cakes, or be a fireman's hat, or an item to tap out rhythms and sound.
▶ Old clothing and pieces of cloth (to use as a wrap-around) can transform role-based imaginary play.
▶ A basket of ribbons may be used to wrap a stick, make a mobile, swaddle a baby doll, create a flow of ribbon as a child's runs.
▶ A piece of cloth or plastic sheeting may be a mat to sit on, or put on the side of a mound to create a water slide, or an item to roll up in and keep warm, or to use as a cape.

- ▶ Tools such as hammers can be used to hammer a nail into bare earth, a piece of polystyrene and then progressing onto soft timber (often evolving into far more complex projects such as building a cubby house); shovels can be used to dig a hole, plants for planting a garden or building a watercourse.
- ▶ A rope can be used to tie to a tree, be a skipping rope, or an item on a lawn to balance on or jump over.
- ▶ An old large timber crate can be a place for hiding in, a cradle for dolls, a sheltered space for visiting animals during the day or for setting on its side and jumping off.

The more varied the loose parts, the more creative, sustained and varied the play responses will be.

Large items tend to be teacher-led. These can be obvious such as a second ladder to lead up to a play platform, or trestles when they want a plank to be higher. But it can also be subtle, such as shifting a plank slightly to introduce challenge. Teachers need to be aware of safety.

The placement of smaller items can be as simple as a basket of dress-up clothes positioned next to the play platform, or a water trough filled on a hot day.

There are also many instances of child choice, for example, when older children are encouraged to access the stored items or when a child uses stones or logs or prunes branches to construct a bridge.

8.3 Junk or recycled materials

Junk is a cheap and varied source of play materials. As it has no set use, junk can be incorporated into a wide range of play. Its uniqueness will frequently inspire children's imagination and they will show ingenuity as they alter, change and adapt items to suit play, enjoying the opportunity to develop and follow through ideas, often on a large scale. They can destroy junk with impunity; for instance when involved in an activity such as unscrewing an old clock, their curiosity is given free rein to find out what is inside and learn a little of how it works. Also, if a course of action during play is unsuccessful, the frustration felt could be less than would be experienced if it were an irreplaceable object.

The play potential of junk material is unlimited, but what is required is the imaginative, innovative ideas and persistence of a discerning teacher. Safety is a key factor in selection. The teacher must be constantly aware of potential hazards such as falls from high crates, cuts from nails and staples, inhalation of small polystyrene beads and blocked ears, poisoning from liquid residue in containers, and cuts and grazes from harsh surfaces. Teachers are on a steep learning curve when using loose parts as this type of play enables children to learn through taking calculated risks.

Some ideas for junk materials for loose items in the playground include:

- ▶ solid timber crates for cubbies and climbing: if used for climbing they should be no more than 1000mm high x 1500mm long as this allows easy reach and supervision by adults;
- ▶ old wooden drink crates for climbing that are solid and have had any gaps filled to prevent a child's foot slipping through;
- ▶ rubber tyres,can be used for climbing equipment or for placing jouncing boards on; they must however, be checked prior to usage to ensure that tyres with protruding steel in worn tyres are not used;
- ▶ an old mattress covered in vinyl, with strong stitched vinyl handles, for jumping and breaking falls;
- ▶ polystyrene cartons to store equipment for dramatic play or used as a motivational tool when learning how to use a hammer and a nail. Careful selection of the polystyrene is needed to ensure that it does not crumble too readily or play into the hands of overzealous safety concerns through the presence of a teacher who provides support and clarification;
- ▶ cardboard rolls can be used in various ways: narrow fabric ones for dramatic play, and large form work cylinders as cubbies and as tunnels for children to crawl through;

Figure 8.2 Kathy's House Family Day Care, Brisbane Australia: family day care centre with masterly use of recycled materials

▶ cardboard or polystyrene cartons: small, solid ones for sitting in, or storing equipment, and large washing machine and refrigerator cartons for cubbies and painting;
▶ air-filled inner tubes for climbing, balancing and sitting in, or for rolling along;
▶ plumbers' PVC off-cuts for digging pits and water play;
▶ an old conveyor belt for use as a water slide or as part of a watercourse;
▶ sacks filled with crumpled newspaper to make punching bags, or as an aid to dramatic play;
▶ a disused fire hose for dramatic play or as a challenging rope to swing on;
▶ an old garden hose and short pieces of plastic tubing to aid water and dramatic play;
▶ small low log rounds to step on or to move about;
▶ old curtains with metal fittings removed and old washable rugs for dramatic play;
▶ lightweight plastic tarpaulin fabric to use as a temporary frictionless slide with water on slopes in summer;
▶ for sand play, old saucepans, spoons, frying-pans, ice-cream and other plastic containers;
▶ for water play, plastic bottles cut in half to produce a funnel and container, sponges, corks, items that float, plastic tubing, containers to pour from or that have been pierced with holes to make sieves, balloon whisks, plunger tops and bottles from laundries;
▶ for dramatic play, old caps, hats and helmets, steering wheels, cushions, small baskets, stools and old telephones;
▶ for older children, small-scale junk that can be pulled apart using screw drivers, pliers, spanners and tweezers;

- ▶ sawn-down tree trunks with only the stumps of large boughs remaining for building cubbies and linking equipment to;
- ▶ various colours of old electrical wiring to lash items together;
- ▶ water-based paints or coloured chalk to embellish many junk creations.

8.4 Movable equipment

There is a variety of commercially manufactured equipment that can provide a valuable addition to the loose parts on offer for children's play and learning. If there are enterprising parents or carers with the right skills then some of the items below could also be made using recycled materials. What to choose will depend on local availability and need, although play spaces should include at least some of the following:

- ▶ trestles: for younger children to climb on, to link planks at flat and angled levels, as a one-off item or as a completed obstacle course with other materials;
- ▶ rigid planks: these are the variety of planks that are invaluable for linking up low trestles to create obstacle courses; at other times children may place a cloth over the top between two higher climbing trestles and planks to create a hidey space underneath;
- ▶ jouncing boards: long, low planks designed specifically to be placed between two trestles so that children have the opportunity of walking on a giving surface; toddlers particularly enjoy this use when holding on to a teacher's hand as they learn to jump up and down and off;
- ▶ ladders with cleated or hookshaped ends: a tool for climbing up to a deck, for clambering on a different surface between two trestles;
- ▶ cleated ramp plank: these provide a further extension to ladder and plank use, such as creating a bridge;
- ▶ outdoor modular blocks: these are the perfect example of open-ended loose parts that can be used over a number of years if sufficient space and additions to the block collection are included. In children's ever-present imaginations other loose parts are often incorporated such as dolls in an imaginary castle, site of a cave, a tunnel for the aircraft or just a place to get away;
- ▶ wheeled carts/trolleys: these can be loaded with blocks for carting back to storage, for wheeling a load of sand toys, a load of dirt, seeds for the garden or to feed the animals;
- ▶ water trough: this will need a variety of smaller loose parts or junk items to enhance water play such as funnels, jugs, colanders, floating toys, bottles, bowls, sieves, small hand pumps, small water wheels, plastic tubing and sponges;
- ▶ carpentry bench: this will need a variety of additional loose parts to be effective, such as hammers, sandpaper, pieces of wood or pieces of polystyrene and so on. Careful selection of the polystyrene is needed to ensure that it does not crumble too readily, e.g. extruded polystyrene;
- ▶ a selection of buckets – small and large, some with spouts to assist with pouring.

Clearly the adventurous use of recycled materials requires an observant and supportive teacher who will encourage and explain usage to children and assist with comprehension of risk when needed.

8.5 Storage sheds

The siting and design of a shed for storing loose parts is critical. The shape and size of an outdoor shed depends on the number of children and whether older children (3+ years) have independent access to items. If storage sheds are to be effective their location, space and size should be considered carefully during the master planning process. These storage sheds should be seen not as a place for the placement of junk from other parts of the centre but as the storage facility for valuable play items.

As they get older, children need to be actively engaged in selecting, putting away and tidying up. At best, this activity expands their capacity for decision-making, time management and assists with developing a sense of responsibility. Older children may well develop negotiation skills over choice of items, as well as planning and/or creative skills as they move from solo to shared play concepts and activities.

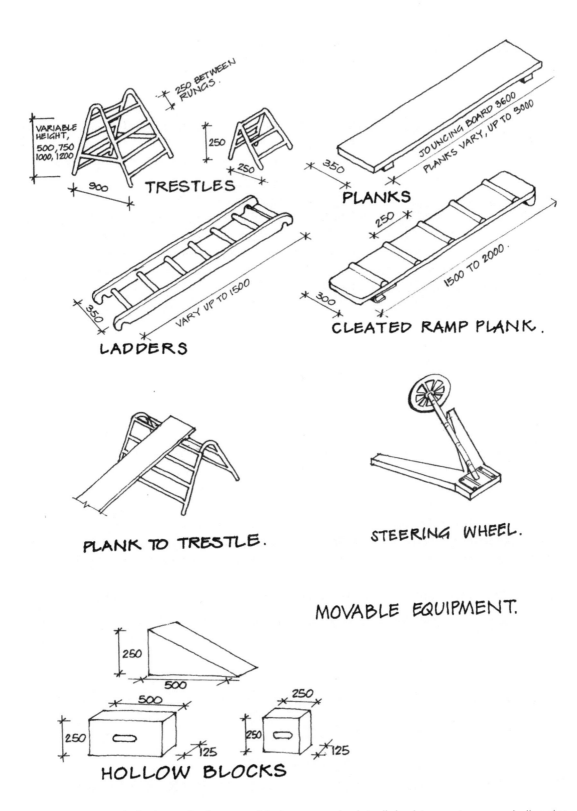

Figure 8.3 Trestles chand planks and other portable items can be interlinked to create more challenging obstacle courses. A selection of large hollow blocks can be used to create and build cubby houses, roads etc

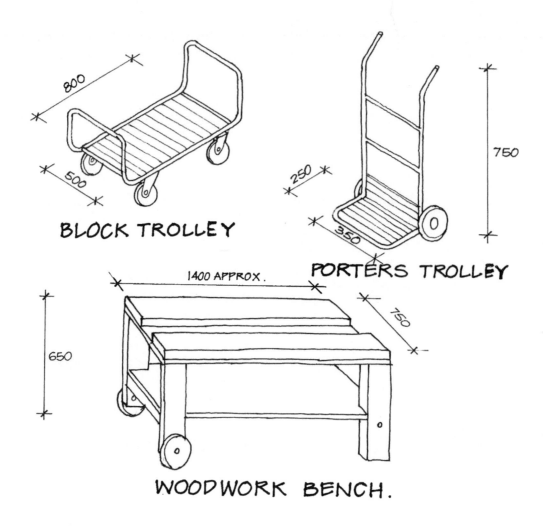

BLOCK TROLLEY

800

500

PORTERS TROLLEY

250

350

750

WOODWORK BENCH.

1400 APPROX.

650

750

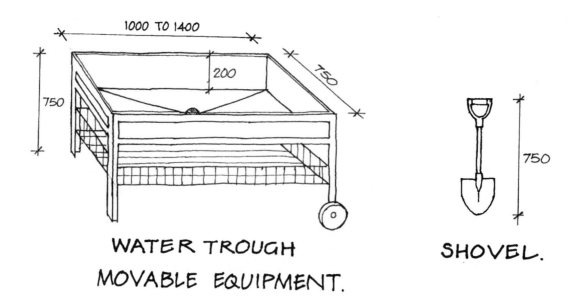

WATER TROUGH
MOVABLE EQUIPMENT.

1000 TO 1400

200

750

750

SHOVEL.

750

Figure 8.4 Movable play items can be kept in storage sheds. They offer a wide range of potential play and can be used to transport equipment by staff and children throughout the playground

Figure 8.5 C&K Tarragindi War Memorial Kindergarten, Brisbane Australia. Child accessible storage sheds designed for 3- to 5-year-olds to help them select, set up and put away equipment. Designed to ensure safe access and enable wheeled toys to be stored on the lower shelves

Systematic storage can enable ready access to a wide variety of loose parts. However, care needs to be taken with selection as bulky items will dominate the storage space and limit the variety of play materials that can be provided. Therefore, consideration should always be given to purchasing a wider range of smaller items.

In terms of planning, shed(s) are better placed near to a point of intended use. This applies particularly to the heavy planks, ladders and so on needed for the active play area. The smaller or tighter the playground space is, the more dependent on loose parts the users will be.

Shed(s) can be freestanding or constructed as part of the building. Consider more than one storage shed; for example, separate storage for different age groups, or separate storage on each level (especially if an embankment is involved), or perhaps separate storage for specific use items (like gardening, animal house). Avoid lightweight aluminum sheds that in practice can be blown away and often cannot support the desired well designed solid shelving.

8.5.1 Design considerations

Consider the following:

▶ Select a slim, rectangular shed with a wide opening on one side as generally this is a more effective use of space and has less 'dead space' than a squat or bulky shed. Slim sheds are easier to erect along a fence line or in a corner, so that there are no supervisory problems for the staff. A shed can be as narrow as 1–1.5m (more like a cupboard) and still be effective.

CHILD ACCESSIBLE STORAGE SHED.

Figure 8.6 C&K Tarragindi War Memorial Kindergarten, Brisbane Australia. Child accessible storage sheds designed for 3- to 5-year-olds to help them select, set up and put away equipment. Designed to ensure safe access and enable wheeled toys to be stored on the lower shelves

▶ Placement of shelving needs to be carefully considered against anthropometric data leaving a lower shelf for wheeled toys to be readily placed and accessed by children; heavy planks in line with staff members' hips; and higher shelves for items stored in clear plastic containers to enable ready access.

▶ Wide hooks for hanging items within the shed will contribute towards effective use of available space.

▶ Make floors damp-proof (usually concrete) and constructed with a slight (1:100 fall) slope out of the shed to an adjoining draining facility. Ensure the floor is continuous with an extended paved or concrete area in front of the shed to minimise dirt tracking.

▶ Position a tap close to the shed, and preferably near an adjoining garden bed, so that the water is not wasted, for easy washing down of items before storage.

▶ Supplement natural ventilation and light if required, especially in dank climates or reduced daylight.

▶ Consider locks, window grilles and a motion-sensitive light. If the shed is also used for maintenance items such as lawn mowers, consideration should always be given to a divider partition and a separate door due to the potential risk to children.

CHAPTER 9

Playgrounds for toddlers and babies

9.1 Why outside play is important for toddlers and babies

Babies and toddlers are usually defined as being 0 to 1 year and 1 to 2.5 years during what is the most rapid years of development where they change from supine babies to crawling babies to newly mobile upright toddlers. Because of this major developmental change their range and form of activities will vary enormously during this time. Each of these stages can also vary individually between children.

This is a vital time when the foundation of competency and resiliency skills needed throughout life are laid down. Their experience of life expands through exploration which enhances their mastery of skills. Anita Rui Olds (2001) states that:

> Environments are potent purveyors of stimulation, information, and affect, and infants and toddlers, in particular, are sensitive to all the quality of aspects of a setting; its movements, sounds, volumes, textures, visual and aesthetic vibrations, forms, colour, and rhythms.

An outdoor area is ideally suited to providing opportunities for learning-through-play but only if the physical environment is appropriate both in design and in it can assist teaching practice. Given children's incomplete mastery of their bodies, teachers observation and supervision needs to be supportive, physically and psychologically, and capable of assessing when an individual is ready to move on to a new developmental challenge.

The developmental changes in this period are astounding. The importance of this cannot be underestimated: it is now that future competencies and preferences are established. A baby or toddler who is introduced into a world of discovery can often be far more independent and quite different to an individual whose domain is a cramped facility with few opportunities for exploration or extending their gross motor activities and who has to compete for the same play opportunities. Children need space. They need sensory input. They need challenges that they can realistically achieve – that is, the zone of proximal development as described by the Russian thinker Lev Vygotsky (Newman and Holzman, 2014). And they need a setting which allows activities that provide them with a 'scaffold' for learning, including risky behaviour that may be perceived as being unacceptable by over concerned adults.

Baby/toddlers need comfort and support preferably from one consistent teacher. The setting for this age group needs to ensure a soft inviting space with a supportive teacher with a subtle variety of changes in the environment which will offer of potential activities.

Within the toddler phase, individuals will become independent, often fiercely so, rushing unsteadily to whatever catches their attention. They tend to use many small, repetitive actions: up/down movements, splashing or moving sideways along a bench. Much of a toddler's play is motivated by curiosity: with their single-mindedness their task of exploration and discovery will leave them pulling, dumping, switching with often a marked indifference to the consequences of this with other children as they assert their independence. Yet quick changes can occur as they seek support, be passive or wanting to sit down and observe. Play can be varied as busy exploration as they undertake actions like turning on taps and access switches and pulling things down on top of themselves can happen. Their play is a serious and compelling business for them and much of it is egocentric. They do not want others to intrude and will push other toddlers aside as they determinedly go their own way. They will seldom play in groups, unless the activity is teacher-led.

However, mutual play evolves as toddlers watch, copy, play alongside one another or make brief contact with their peers. It is essential to remember that an effective outdoor playground is one which offers visual delight with sensory richness and small subtle changes in the environment backed by the use of loose parts and teacher understanding and support.

The exploration and expansion of activities within their setting and with other children is ongoing and lays the foundations for layering of experiences. Having no access to a suitable playground is in effect depriving them of vital experiences during their pivotal period of development.

Figure 9.1 Kathy's House Family Day Care, Brisbane Australia: this creative setting uses a recycled laundry tub with access to water. A variety of different plants add sensory richness

9.2 Planning for baby and toddler playgrounds

Because an outdoor area provides learning experiences that often cannot be achieved elsewhere a degree of familiarity and compatible play items will be less daunting for this age group. Yet it must offer different opportunities and should be a careful blend of new, natural experiences and some familiar manmade or junk items. The selection of these items needs to be sensitively carried out to due to the markedly different needs of babies vs toddlers. Outdoors must offer a varied form of play to what is available indoors.

There are similarities between planning a playground for older children, and for babies and toddlers. However, the following planning elements need special consideration.

9.2.1 Location

Planning an early childhood centre should always consider the location of toddlers and babies in the context of the whole site and the interaction to adjoining spaces. A location near busy roads and freeways, with car fumes and ongoing noise, undermines the play offer, to say nothing of the risk of toxicity and even injuries from such close proximity to cars – it is staggering how often this does occur.

Layout

Preferably the design provides a separate playground for toddlers and babies adjoining from the main space. This will be an area where they do not have to compete with older, more agile

Figure 9.2 Capital Hill Early Childhood Centre, Canberra: natural materials with varying textures are carefully laid out to ensure they are readily accessible to newly mobile children

children for their play opportunities. Developmentally however, it provides the advantage of children being able to watch and often copy the patterns of older children and enjoy the beginning of early socialisation with different age groups. It is essential that full separation does not occur. It is often the observation and interaction with older children through a fence and selected sharing times that is particularly advantageous for social emotional development not only to the younger children but also the older children as this may be their first opportunity to interact with different age groups.

The division between older and younger children should be a subtle definition of space achieved through a low fences or raised garden beds so that children can readily view over, be aware of and have a degree of interaction with older children. In practice as they get older and more competent they will possibly seek to move into the older playground and this should be seen as a developmental plus, and indication that they are ready for more challenging and stimulating settings.

The layout should be very similar to that of the older children's playground, but on a smaller scale, for example with quiet areas, open areas, active areas and natural areas (see design characteristics, Figure 2.1, page 13).

Because toddlers often have a short attention span, the design should assist them to move between activities while also providing items and elements within the space, such as sensory panels, textured surfaces and planting. If it is well designed the interlinking of spaces will allow for a flow of activities between different spaces and help to minimise the risk of conflict with children who are already occupied. For example, a sandpit should not extend directly into an active play space such as a climbing equipment area.

The location and the elements within it should always consider the climatic considerations relevant to the location. Shade sails and shady trees that cover most of the playground are needed in hot climates. The deciduous trees and pergolas covered with flowering vines which offer seasonal sensory patterns in more temperate climates allow for the emergence of the winter sun to warm the outdoor play in winter.

Space

Space for young children should not be underestimated. They need access to open areas, room to crawl, fall, flop onto the group, spaces to push an item, to practice stiff legged gaits that become the running movements later on. A bare minimum of 6sqm per child is needed but preferably more. Good spatial provision will also allow the partial separation of crawling babies and newly mobile toddlers often needed due to the single mindedness of newly upright toddlers. In practice the extent of the potential usage is often underestimated.

Landform

Changing landforms with undulating mounds and/or gently inclined embankments or ramped access pathways are the sorts of landforms that prompt children to explore. They also offer the opportunity to take on challenge, the enjoyment of viewing things from a height, the pleasure (as skills develop) of sliding down as well as crawling up. For example, gentle embankments with ramped access for crawling up and down or a slide from a height of approximately 1.5 to a maximum of 1.8m are not beyond the realm of 18 months to 2-year-olds, who enjoy the challenge of changing height, the thrill of the movement of sliding down (slides to be set well into the embankment with high sides to grip onto) and provide the challenge and thrill of movement without the risk of vertical falls. Subtly of design with many opportunities for discovery are needed with the dominance of a major challenging force or structure inhibiting the overall diversity of the play experience. With designs like this it also makes it easy for the teacher to provide the essential support and observation needed.

Figures 9.3 & 9.4 Tugulawa Early Education, Brisbane Australia: the junction between the senior and junior playground shows a level of social interaction that can occur between younger and older children. Low level tables are included for setting up play equipment

Interrelationship of space

The final assessment is that it is a part of the main playground but is a very clearly defined separate area specifically for the younger children. Often a sandpit provision can be an extension of the older children's playground area with a divider bench in between to assist with the socialisation that close proximity to older children provides. Nooks and crannies, small mounds, embankments with ramps with stepped sides or handrails when provided have been actively used by all children of this age group.

Partial separation of these areas between the older and younger children can easily be achieved with items as simple as:

▶ a raised garden bed to a height of 500mm;
▶ a low fence with vertical slats with a smooth continuous plank on the top to a height of 600mm to act as a surface for children to pull themselves into an upright position to view beyond;
▶ flat top play decks with infill railings approximately 500–600mm high to enable socialisation and shared play to occur between the young children and older children in the adjoining play space;
▶ provision of upright posts with slot in panels made of Perspex of varying colours and textures – a surface which has multiple uses of stimulating an upright position, sensory contact, viewing and interaction with children in the adjoining play space.

Inside and outside

As the age and skill levels, sleep patterns and group sizes need to vary to accommodate the demanding changes that are occurring it is essential that the inside and outside areas are interlinked to a level that a crawling baby, nearly upright toddlers and even those beginning to run can move between the inside and outside areas. According to the developmental needs of the children, the teacher can run part of the programme inside. For example, when the busier children are outside the quieter children can be inside or alternatively when the older children are inside the quieter children have time to explore outside in a gentle way. To achieve this, the following needs to be provided:

▶ a flat continuous surface from the playroom out to the playground to minimise tripping and to allow independent crawling and walking;
▶ shade provision throughout the year for hotter climates or through seasonal provision e.g. deciduous vines in cooler climates;
▶ locating of the transition area which provides a viewing point to the rest of the playground to enable exploration of children and non-intrusive observation and support by staff can readily occur.

Back-up materials

Water access to key play areas e.g. sandpit, verandah surfaces, for watering plants and hosing the lawn at the end of the day.

Loose parts

Provision of loose parts requires careful selection by teacher based on needs and patterns of children's behaviour being noted to identify if they are seeking extension. Small items that respond to making a sound, larger items such as mats to lie on, foam rubber tyre moulds for lying on and leaning across. Natural materials however, should abound e.g. small rings of timber, small pieces of a bamboo fence, smooth logs are often used for children to pull themselves to an upright position (refer to loose parts in Section 8, page 88).

Storage

The rapidly changing developmental needs of children mean that storage needs to be carefully selected and preferably a separate storage area provided adjoining the toddler/baby playground. This success of the storage shed needs to take into account the size of the items to be used within the area to ensure appropriate shelving is included (refer to storage in Section 8.5 on pages 92–96).

Planting

Plants for shade, to accommodate different seasons are needed not only for older children but also for younger children's playgrounds. Selection of plants needs care to ensure that small items that can be poked into ears and mouths are not included (refer to planting in Section 3.6 on pages 32–33).

9.2.2 Ambience

The ambience of a baby and toddler playground can be characterised as 'difference with sameness' – a child's exploration and development of ideas needs reassurance through both the teaching and the setting. It needs familiar items, a recognition of space and a focal point within the play area such as a seating area under a large tree where the teacher can sit on a boulder and be with the children.

The playground needs a few distinctive areas that the children can see from every angle to get their bearings and the reassurance of knowing that, while they may only just be crawling or walking with a stiff-legged gait, they can get back to the point where they started.

9.2.3 Adaptability

The viability of any setting and fixture within the playground depends on the capacity to be adapted and altered in a multitude of ways. The setting needs to be designed in a manner that it is open ended through the use of loose parts, while the permanence is provided in the setting and the fixtures within it. Initial planning should include a separate storage shed for toddler and baby equipment either immediately in or adjoining the playground and of a design that will not cut into or create blind viewing spots within the playground so that teachers can easily view and access play items.

9.3 Design characteristics

There are six key zones, described below, that should be considered when designing baby and toddler playgrounds.

9.3.1 Hub area

This area – a sandpit, a paved area – needs to be visible from every part of the playground. Often a tree, pergola or a shade structure is used as a 'comfort beacon'. The surface is very important and should be easy to clean and to drain so that messy play can take place here. Plant vines that flower at different times of the year, and install wind chimes and a chain and carabiner hook so that different items can be suspended from the ceiling of a shelter space.

9.3.2 Natural play area

This is not always a defined area, because the play can be distributed over the total area. Natural play lends itself to taking place along fence lines or adjacent to quieter play areas. This play could involve a hidey hole under drooping leaves, peep holes through vines, a herb garden in a raised garden bed, a variety of surfaces, bare earth, sand, sensory pathways with gentle patterns (for example imprinted leaves, pressed ripple iron or marbles set into the surface) and simple versions of some of the elements they will experience in the main playground in later years, such as small, shallow wading pools.

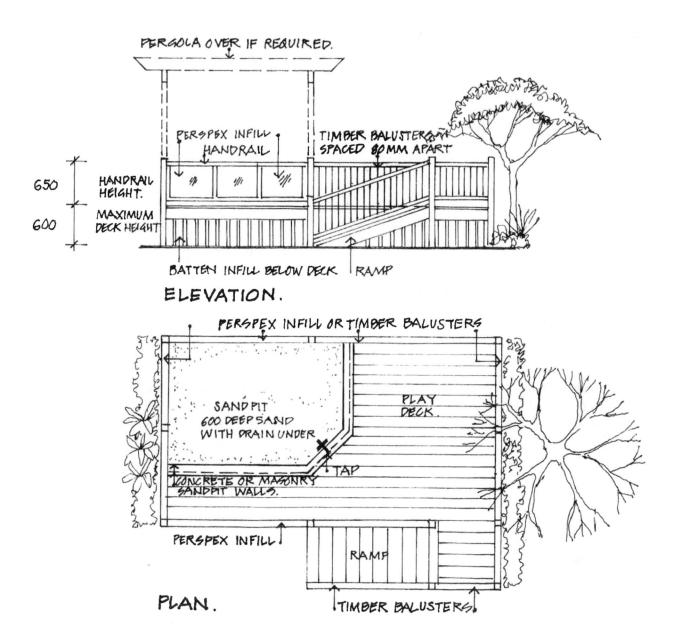

PERGOLA OVER IF REQUIRED.

PERSPEX INFILL HANDRAIL

TIMBER BALUSTERS SPACED 80 MM APART

650 HANDRAIL HEIGHT.

600 MAXIMUM DECK HEIGHT

BATTEN INFILL BELOW DECK   RAMP

ELEVATION.

PERSPEX INFILL OR TIMBER BALUSTERS

SAND PIT 600 DEEP SAND WITH DRAIN UNDER

PLAY DECK.

TAP

CONCRETE OR MASONRY SANDPIT WALLS.

PERSPEX INFILL

RAMP

PLAN.

TIMBER BALUSTERS

Figure 9.5 Raised toddler playdeck with sandpit

9.3.3 Open play area

This needs to support movement at speed and enable toddlers to develop from a stiff-legged gait to running. It can incorporate a mound or a low embankment or an encircling pathway that extends around the periphery of the area to provide a link to all sections of the play area that children of all skill levels can use. Wheeled toys can be provided to enhance this play.

9.3.4 Quiet area

These are small spaces where toddlers and babies can retreat and observe other children with the comfort of knowing that others are around, such as:

▶ small cubbies;
▶ sunken pits under decks with sufficient head clearance at a minimum of 1.5m for toddlers to enter and hide;
▶ paved areas surrounded by boulders;

- ▶ a bench around the base of a tree where they can pull themselves up and side-step around;
- ▶ a space where the teacher can put out soft mats, cushions, foam blocks to section an area for crawling babies from the heady activities of a newly mobile toddler yet to develop the understanding of how intrusive their play may be to the crawling baby
- ▶ sandpits that babies and toddlers can access themselves whether it be a sunken pit with a wide sweeping edge and a bull-nosed brick edge that they can crawl in and out by themselves or a low timber deck with a low railing fence around it and a ramp for crawling up and down;
- ▶ clumps of bamboo or willow arches, hidey spaces and weaving pathways.

9.3.5 Active play area

The primary challenge for toddlers is to 'get somewhere', and so this area needs to provide a destination such as a play platform, a swing (with appropriate barriers), an embankment or a mound. In terms of actual design, the area will need stairs (of different types), ramps, perhaps a slide built into the bank, handrails or ropeways to hold on to for a gentle incline or embankment, or even just a slope to roll down.

9.3.6 Barriers or transition spaces

The design of the barriers between the older and younger children's play spaces should enable observation as well as social contact, for example low fences, raised garden beds, low gates with a side opening away from the toddler and baby playground can be used to create integrated space at the teacher's discretion. The opening/latch should be on the opposite side of the low gate in the older children's area (if adjoining) so that access can controlled by the teacher. Should children attempt to climb this low fence it should be seen as a developmental plus and a clear message that the children are needing more challenging play opportunities: perhaps a time to open the gate and see who moves.

CHAPTER 10

Playgrounds for children with special needs

10.1 Why outside play is important for children with special needs

One of the key areas of difficulty for children with special needs or specific learning difficulties is a delay in the connections between the neural pathways. Constant reinforcement of activities to stimulate these neural pathways is essential if a learner with special education needs or specific learning difficulties is to achieve his or her potential. The brain reacts to the environment as it learns from experience. A stimulating environment encourages network formation and 'results in the improvement of the brain's ability to react, learn and memorise – its intelligence' (Portwood 2000). For example, proprioception (the awareness of where our limbs are in space) affects many children with learning difficulties such as ADHD, dyspraxia and dyslexia. The sensitive receptors that react to the amount of contraction or stretch our muscles undergo when moving inform our brain which records it in our memory system. This kinaesthetic mapping is an essential part of developing good gross motor skills, which in turn produce more sophisticated fine motor skills essential for learning, both in the classroom and generally in life skills. The vestibular system also provides us with information regarding the direction and speed of movement. It enables us to develop good muscle tone and balance. If the proprioceptive and vestibular systems do not function effectively a child will appear clumsy and uncoordinated – a feature prevalent in a child with dyspraxia.

The nature of physical play is directly related to the child's level of motor control. In most children this is an area of voluntary movement, but for those children with special needs this is not so clearly defined. Activities such as weaving in and out of obstacles, combining swift changes of movement and direction, following a sequence of activities and keeping balance are an essential

Figure 10.1 Infants playground, Mater Dei School, Camden, New South Wales. This school for children with an intellectual disability has been designed to allow independent safe access and enjoyment

part of achieving fluidity of movement. Playground activities that incorporate the use of large muscle groups (coordination of arms, legs, head and trunk) leading to improvement in control of small muscles groups (balance in the feet or hand grasping, which is involved in large movements such as climbing) form part of a child's developmental milestones. Manipulative skills such as pouring take place through sand and water play; this is where loose items combine spatial judgement, movement control and clear separate roles for both hands. The use of each tool often requires practice for children with impaired motor control.

There is often conflict between child safety and development of these fine motor skills and supported practice may be required, particularly where a sequence of activities is required. A well-designed playground does much to support the teacher's role by facilitating one-to-one contact, observation and support. A playground that incorporates plenty of multisensory stimulation will improve the integration of skills such as spatial awareness, body image, interaction and self-esteem. Equally, it is important to include tranquil areas where a child who has difficulty in assimilating numerous activities has the opportunity for 'down time'.

Above all children with special educational needs require more time to organise their thoughts, actions and responses. They may have devised strategies to avoid difficult tasks so it is important to show appreciation of the things that they are good at, while encouraging them to challenge their limitations – giving plenty of support and affirmation along the way. This is especially important in younger children where self-esteem seems to rely more on success than on doing the same activity as everyone else.

Children with special needs have a critical need and right to play as an essential means of maximising their potential. Integration, not segregation, is the need of most children with special needs. For most children this is best done when they are integrated into a well-planned and equipped children's centre playground. It allows them to be seen primarily as individuals in their own right and only secondarily as children with special needs.

The early childhood centre is often the first and only opportunity some of these children have of being fully integrated. If handled well, it will provide them with important insights and an expanded view of life. It may also help in part to prevent further deterioration of existing abilities and help them compensate for skills that are unlikely to be fully developed. For others whose special needs are less acute, it is an important stepping stone, the first opportunity towards integration and independence in life.

Outside play gives children with special needs an opportunity to be treated more like their more able peers. Indeed, Leland G Shaw (1987) observes that:

> Well-designed playgrounds with ample space where planning has been carried out by informed parties with a deep understanding of children's play and development... are the most effective spaces for accommodating a markedly varied range of skills and needs that can occur within any group of children, let alone those with special needs.

In outdoor play children with special needs can imitate, model behaviour on what they observe and, like other children, play on the periphery of groups before integrating with smaller and larger groups. Their level of development and type of special need will have a bearing on how fully they become involved. For many, peer group pressure will be an incentive, and it may also make them aware for the first time that they are different in some ways. This realisation can be part of an early process of growing acceptance. It need not be a negative experience, but rather one of reaching a reality that will help them move on to acquire skills to accommodate and handle their needs, social and otherwise.

It is not possible to meet all the play objectives and goals of children with special needs in an early childhood centre, but a wide range of these children can be, and are, integrated. It may take a child with severe cerebral palsy many months to learn, for example, to climb a low timber bridge – but this may well also signal a whole new level of independence and be a cause of celebration for everyone at the centre.

Children with different forms of Asperger's actively seek and need settings that allow them to play alone, retreat and observe. Marked variations are exhibited with Asperger's depending on factors such as the form, severity, the level of early intervention, support, experience and continuity of the teacher and the acceptance, support and level of consistent loving handling.

It is also a learning experience for the other children: sometimes their questions, which may seem blunt to an adult, show an honest curiosity that will help them, often quickly and readily, accept people with special needs, not only at this stage but throughout their lives.

10.2 Planning outside play spaces for children with special needs

The first priority must always be that the playground is for all children: it is a place for fun, socialisation and to expand skills, and focuses on the whole child and the integration of children with special needs where possible.

Consider what features to include for children with special needs against the amount of space available. The dominance of one element that will only support a couple of children can be costly for the other children at the centre, and may raise questions as to whether the physical environment can truly support children with special needs.

In reality, a well-designed large open space with nooks and crannies, varied spaces for setting up play, a variety of planting, water, access points and lookout areas, as previously described in this book, will serve the majority of children well.

10.2.1 General design considerations

While it may not be possible to satisfy all of the following, paying attention to as many as possible will help to create inclusive playgrounds:

▶ Provide a playground with a dominance of open-ended items that will invite a variety of different forms of play, especially when combined with loose parts.
▶ Offer graduated challenges to encourage, and not threaten, a child, following assessment and evaluation of each child's play needs.
▶ Use unstructured natural play materials such as sand and water, which can give a child an easily-won sense of achievement and creative enjoyment as they play.
▶ Make plentiful loose parts available: these can be readily modified to ensure that the playground can meet varied skill levels and provide the ongoing challenge to stimulate new levels of development.
▶ Focus on providing a sensory-rich environment that will arouse the interest of many children with special needs, and that will allow them to play at their own interest and skill level and to adapt elements as part of developing more creative uses of a setting.
▶ Provide settings that can be modified to allow children in wheelchairs to participate in dramatic play, such as playing out life roles and fantasies within a group setting.
▶ Ensure that quiet spaces are provided as children with special needs are more likely to tire, and to need to retreat and rest for a while, or just wish to observe others at play.
▶ Take special care to balance challenge with risk: children with special needs require challenge just as other children do – however, the amount must be carefully monitored to ensure they are not inhibited or put at greater risk because of the limitations they may already have.

10.3 Design considerations

There are some specific points to note when considering suitable playgrounds for children with special needs. Consult local standards for more detailed requirements.

10.3.1 Access

▶ Layout of areas should maximise access for children with physical special needs to enable them to pass easily from the building to the play areas, and from one area to another. This should also help staff teach these children easily and give help when needed.

▶ Include paths to facilitate wheelchair access to the main play areas, enabling children to reach the areas on their own. Once there, a child can be assisted out of a wheelchair and supported to sit in a sandpit or a cart, or helped onto a slide, to give her or him a better opportunity of hands-on play. Paths will save staff having to carry a child over a long distance, so the process is quicker and less arduous. Care must be taken with placement, and the number of paths should be kept at a minimum so that the flow or extension of other children's play is not inhibited or restricted, while a child using a wheelchair is still enabled to reach all major points in the playground.

▶ Entry paths and gates shared by groups of children should be at least 1m wide, and have a firm, non-slip surface with a crosswise camber not in excess of 1:100. The maximum gradient for easy access by children on foot is 1 in 14 and is best suited to short distances of approximately 1 to 1.5m, where children can build up speed before reaching the rise. Long ramps for self-propelled access should have a lower gradient.

▶ To signal a physical change in the setting (for example a door, ramp or steps) use a different pattern of bricks in a path, or another surface or a line of bricks in concrete. A rough groove or a surface change adjoining the doorway, or even a few metres ahead as a larger landing pad, can be particularly useful for children with visual or other impairments.

▶ Ramps to aid access in and out of the building should be at least 1m wide, have a hard, slip-resistant surface and a gradient of no more than 1 in 14. Handrails can be added later at relatively little expense.

▶ Design a main access pathway to provide a continuous surface for prams, trolleys and wheelchairs and to assist children with limited mobility. Increase access to other parts of the playground where there are steeper inclines by adding a handrail to the pathway, which will help to extend the skills of all children. Design steps where the tread is about 260mm with evenly spaced risers of no less than 150mm that do not overlap the step to cause tripping. The use of colour or contrasting strips on the edge of steps will assist children or adults with visual impairments.

▶ Adjoining surface materials should be flush to prevent tripping and to aid wheelchair access. Non-slip flat flush surfaces into areas such as cubby houses and storage sheds will enable children with limited mobility to self-select activities more readily.

▶ A flat, hard surface area will enable a child with a physical special need to pull themselves along on a low, flat scooter board.

▶ A mound or embankment with a ramp or gradient of no more than 1 in 12 will facilitate wheelchair access. A flat area at the high point will prevent a wheelchair rolling off and allow a child a rare opportunity of watching from a height others at play. Other children will enjoy the experience of rolling down a mound and gain vestibular stimulation.

▶ A circular concrete tunnel, approximately 2m long and 1m in diameter, wide enough to allow wheelchair access, can be built into a mound. Pad the outer rims to minimise the risk of accidents. A child in a wheelchair will enjoy the sense of enclosure this provides.

10.3.2 Level changes

▶ Level changes should be maintained to help extend gross motor skills for those able to use them. The inclusion of access pathways, slippery slides and other items to accommodate change in level extends the potential usage further.

▶ Provide alternative access and egress points from different levels within the play space and in the process help children to think and manage these challenges independently.

10.3.3 Climbing structures

All children will want to use the climbing structure at some stage and should be given the opportunity. For some, this will be a great challenge and their enjoyment can be enhanced by the following features:

▶ A well-designed movable ramp with a flat, slip-resistant surface and a handrail 600mm high can be attached to a climbing structure.

▶ A well-designed slide with high sides for safety and a flat starting off point with long run-off to slow momentum will give a child with special needs a chance to experience speed and momentum. Ideally, a slide for this purpose will be incorporated into the side of the mound.

▶ Climbing equipment, D-handles and posts can have bright or iridescent colours to aid access for children with visual impairments. When selecting colours, take into consideration children who are colour-blind.

▶ Equipment must be positioned with extra care as many children with special needs have poor perceptual skills and sense of balance.

10.3.4 Swings

Swings that emit a small sound while in use and that are sited well away from the traffic flow supply a warning and assist safe access for children who have visual impairments.

The inclusion of swings with pigtail hooks will more easily help to meet a wide range of children's needs and make swings an open-ended play opportunity. A swing specifically designed for children with disabilities – for example a firm-sided plastic or fibreglass shell connecting ropes to the upper cross-beam and the combination of straps to hold the child's body firmly in place if needed – can be readily used with the inclusion of pigtail hooks.

10.4.5 Sandpit

A sandpit with a raised edge approximately 800mm high will allow for a wheelchair to be sufficiently recessed under it to aid sand play, which is particularly effective when the sandpit is designed into a sloping embankment. A less expensive way of meeting this play provision is to use a large metal trough: the wheelchair can be recessed underneath the trough, allowing the child to extend their arms instead of having to raise them. Less expensive but equally successful solutions can be as simple as a solid high-sided cardboard box placed in the sandpit to support a child in an upright position – this will allow the child a sense of inclusion, eye contact and play at the same level as the other children.

10.4.6 Flying fox

Install a low-level flying fox with braided steel cable and a removable shackle to carry interchangeable assemblies and varied fittings that can meet specific developmental needs of children. Assemblies can range from a rope with a single knot to those that support a child with back support and straps. Mounds at the start and finish will allow for easy access on and off the flying fox. This simple practice provides joy to many children with limited mobility problems.

10.3.7 Planting

▶ Scent: Use a variety of scented plants, each in different areas, to help children who have visual impairments to pinpoint where they are in the playground.

▶ Colour: Use brightly coloured flowers, or a sharp contrast (for example white flowers against dark green leaves) to help provide some visual experience for children who have visual impairments.

▶ Shape and texture: Plant a wide variety of shapes and textures with leaves, flowers, pods and bark to heighten the tactile skills of blind children and the sensory perception of children who have intellectual or physical special needs.

▶ Shade: Shadows can give a child who has visual impairment a perception of where they are in the playground.

▶ Shelter: Provide shade for protection from summer sun, and from glare reduction in areas where children with limited mobility may be playing or sitting for some time.

- ▶ Light: Planting which allows good natural light without glare or too much shade is best for children with visual impairments.
- ▶ Canopy: The inclusion of a pergola with deciduous vines will heighten children's awareness of summer shade and winter sun while providing a visual attraction and a scent which will be a delight to a number of children with disabilities. This will heighten their awareness and enjoyment of the natural environment.
- ▶ Access: A raised flower or window box approximately 600mm above ground level will allow room for a wheelchair to be partially recessed underneath, while the seated child tends, waters and enjoys gardening. A tap should be installed above soil level.
- ▶ Reach: If including a bird feeder in the garden, placing it at a height of 650mm would make it accessible to a child in a wheelchair.
- ▶ Control: A secluded jungle area with aromatic plants and different textures can be made into a nature walk, while a level path made up of a variety of materials, for example log rounds and pebbled paving blocks will stimulate blind children and allow a child in a wheelchair, or one with limited mobility, to progress slowly and steadily.

When planning a new centre remember that the layout of facilities and maximising the amount of outdoor space makes a critical difference to any child, but particularly to those with special needs. It is the spatial provision of an adaptable, open-ended playground that will provide a diversity of play options. Too often the budgetary controls imposed by other disciplines forget the value of this investment. Quality outdoor play space shapes the adults of the future and their sense of purpose and enjoyment in life.

Bibliography

Australian Children's Education & Care Quality Authority (2014) *Guide to the Education and Care Services National Law and the Education and Care Services National Regulations 2011*, ACECAQ: Sydney, pp. 72 and 76.

Ball, D., Gill, T. and Spiegal, B. (2012) *Managing Risk in Play Provision Implentation Guide*, Play England.

Bengtsson, A. (1970) *Environmental Planning for Children's Play*, Crosby Lockwood & Sons Ltd: London.

Buchan, N. (2015) *Children in Wild Nature: A Practical Guide to Nature-Based Practice*, Teaching Solutions: Blairgowie, Australia.

Dattner, R. (1969) *Design for Play*, Van Nostrand Reinhold Company: New York.

Davis, J. (2008) 'What might education for sustainability look like in early childhood? A case for participatory, whole-of-settings approaches', in Pramling Samuelsson, I. and Kaga, Y. (eds) *The Contribution of Early Childhood Education to a Sustainable Society*, UNESCO: Paris.

Davis, J.M. (ed.) (2010) *Young Children and the Environment, Early Education for Sustainability*, Cambridge University Press: New York.

Elliott, S. (2010) cited in J.M. Davis (2010) *Young Children and the Environment, Early Education for Sustainability*, Cambridge University Press: New York.

Gill, T. (2014) *The Play Return*, Children's Play Policy Council.

Greenman, G. (2005) *Caring Spaces, Learning Places: Children's Environments That Work*, Second edition, Exchange Press: USA.

Hurtwood, Lady Allen of (1968) *Planning for Play*, Jarrold and Sons: Norwich.

Jambor, T. (1996) 'Dimensions of play: reflections and directions', closing keynote from XIII IPA World Congress, Espoo, Finland. School of Education, University of Alabama: Birmingham, AL.

Kritchevsky, S. and Prescott, E. with Walling, L. (1977) *Planning Environments for Young Children – Physical Space*, NAEYC: Washington D.C., p. 5.

Lee, O. (2012) '5 Reasons to let your kids play in the dirt', online at http://www.takepart.com/article/2012/03/26/5-reasons-let-your-kids-play-dirt accesssed 15 January 2016.

Louv, R. (2005) *Last Child in the Woods: Saving Our Children from Nature Deficit Disorder?* Algonquin Books, Chapel Hill, a division of Workman Publishing: New York.

Moss, S. (2012) *Natural Childhood*, National Trust: Swindon.

Newman, F. and Holzman, L. (2014) *Lev Vygotsky: Revolutionary Scientist*, Psychology Press: Hove, pp. 44–75.

Nicholson, S. (1968) 'How not to cheat children: the theory of loose parts', *Landscape Architecture*, 62: 30–35.

Portwood, M. (2000) *Understanding Developmental Dyspraxia: A Textbook for Students and Professionals*, David Fulton Publishers: London.

Prescott, E. Jones, E. and Kritchevsky, S. (1988) cited in G. Greenman (2005) *Caring Spaces, Learning Places: Children's Environment's That Work*, Exchange Press Inc., p. 23.

Royal Society for the Prevention of Accidents (2004) *Accidents on Children's Playgrounds*, RoSPA: UK.

Rui Olds, A. (2001) *Child Care Design Guide*, McGraw-Hill Education: USA.

Shaw, L. G. (1987) 'Designing playgrounds for able and disabled children' in Weinstein and David (eds) *Spaces for Children: The Built Environment and Child Development*, Plemum Press: New York & London.

Shell, R. E. (1994) 'A great playground? That's kids' stuff', *Smithsonian Magazine*, July: 78–79.

Trancik, A. and Evans, G. W. (1995) 'Spaces fit for children', *Children Youth and Environments*, 12(3): 43–58.

Walsh, P. (1988) *Early Childhood Playgrounds, planning an outside learning environment*, Pademelon Press: New South Wales.

Walsh, P. (2006) *Best Practice Guidelines in Lutheran Education QLD Early Childhood Physical Environments*, Open Book Publishers: Adelaide.

Warden, C. (2012) *Nature Kindergartens and Forest Schools*, Claire Warden.

I hear & I forget
I see & I remember
I do & I understand

Chinese proverb

Index